Praise for How to Fix a Broken Record

This entertaining and inspiring book is loaded with stories that lead you to the one true source that helps fix and heal the broken records in your life.

DJ Icy Ice, World Famous Beat Junkies and
Power 106 Los Angeles

As a deejay, I have many broken records in need of being fixed. As a person, I have many broken records in need of being fixed. As Amena's husband, I'm honored to walk this journey with her. She dug deep into her own story and put together words for us all. Everybody has a record. Everybody needs to read this book.

Matt "DJ Opdiggy" Owen, deejay and music producer

Amena Brown has a way with words. Whether spoken or written in a book, she speaks to the soul with a *knowing*. She knows the humor in our humanity, but she also knows our hurts. And she *always* points us to a Healer. *How to Fix a Broken Record* is no exception. With characteristic wit and wisdom, Amena invites us into the highs and lows of her own story to help us reflect on our own. Most of all, she reminds us that the soundtrack of our lives can always include a redemption song. Grace has a groove to it, and this book will get you dancing once again. For Joy.

Jo Saxton, speaker, author, cohost of *Lead Stories Podcast*,
and board chair for 3Dmovements

Through being a fan of Amena Brown I've learned that whenever she offers soliloquies on how to make our journey of life better, it's always worth my listen/read. *How to Fix a Broken Record* sure delivers!

Speech, founder of hip-hop group Arrested Development

Amena Brown has a charming way of punching you in the gut while making you feel incredibly loved. It's my favorite kind of human because none of us want to get apathetic, but how fun to be challenged by someone who loves us. Amena is a leader and a friend and a personal inspiration to my life. Enjoy this journey with her.

Jennie Allen, founder of IF: Gathering and author of *Nothing to Prove*

Amena Brown is a brilliant woman who understanding the human condition. As a pastor, I appreciate how she captures the complexities of our humanity. As an artist, I am captured by her imagination and humor. This book is like a counseling session that is part fresh air, part whooping'.

Rev. Sandra Maria Van Opstal, executive pastor of Grace and Peace Community and author of *The Next Worship*

Stories—the sweat and blood and joy of life—are what bring us to the table with each other. Amena Brown lives this reality and invites us to remember our own stories, our own songs, in this beautiful life-soundtrack of a book. Read it, and through the raw and honest stories of Amena Brown's life, you'll begin to sing the songs of God over your own life, over your own story, over your own journey.

Kaitlin B. Curtice, Native American author, speaker, worship leader, and author of *Glory Happening*

Amena Brown has been a good friend of mine for years. She is a voice in my life I trust because she means what she says and says what she means. Her words are laced with kindness and truth, honest reflection and humor. You're going to find a lot of the things Jesus talked in this book, and you'll want to do more than just agree with them; you'll want to do something about them.

Bob Goff, Chief Balloon Inflator, Love Does

How to Fix a Broken Record reads like the liner notes of a favorite album, chapters replacing tracks, with favorites you will return to and rediscover.

Kathy Khang, author and speaker

Amena Brown is the Issa Rae of the Christian market. This is a clever, honest, witty book that I am glad to share with my mentees.

Natasha Sistrunk Robinson, author of *Mentor for Life*

I've spent years speaking with Amena Brown at events across the country. I'm always left with the thought that more people need to hear more of her ideas. With this book, they finally can in a fresh new way. The journey is never easy, but Amena never pulls punches and delivers with laughs, tears and honesty.

Jon Acuff, *New York Times* bestselling author of *Finish*

Amena Brown has a creative way of taking readers on a nostalgia journey through life and lessons learned. *How to Fix a Broken Record* is an ingenious and fresh approach to womanhood and growing up in a complex world. This book will make you laugh and reflect simultaneously. By the end, you will invite all your girlfriends over for a reading and slumber party.

Tasha Morrison, Be the Bridge founder and president

This is an incredibly moving book. Amena's honesty inspires us to be more honest with ourselves, and to find a new groove of our own in the process.

> **Mike McHargue,** author of *Finding God in the Waves* and cohost of *The Liturgists Podcast*

Quick-witted, beautifully original, and refreshingly honest, Amena Brown has given this generation an inspiring and timely gift. *How to Fix a Broken Record* is a must-read for anyone looking to feel less alone, be free of lies holding them back, and find confidence in who God uniquely made them to be.

> **Hosanna Poetry,** spoken word artist and author of *I Have a New Name*

As only she can, Amena Brown shares witty, creative, and transparent stories that remind us of our need to fully embrace our own humanity. This book will take you on a hilarious journey toward the growth of deeper relationships, greater self-awareness, and genuine soul healing.

> **Rev. Jonathan E.L. Brooks,** senior pastor of Canaan Community Church, Chicago

Amena Brown's book reads like an unhurried conversation over coffee. She shares vulnerably and offers insight and wisdom on crucial elements in life: relationships, navigating the terrain of becoming an adult without losing your soul, womanhood, ethnicity, identity, and voice. Her book dedication alone is worth the price of the entire book. Journey with her through the pages, and come out on the other side with principles to apply to all aspects of life and relationships.

> **Vivian Mabuni,** speaker and author of *Warrior in Pink*

How to Fix a Broken Record is authentic and soul-baring. Amena Brown is brilliant in how she takes us on a journey of her life. Her readers will relate and engage. She is Beyoncé, and this book is Lemonade.

Jovanie Smith, young adult & mission deployment coordinator for The Salvation Army

How to Fix a Broken Record has become a go-to read for me. I've found so much encouragement in the ways that Amena Brown honestly talks about the joys and challenges of moving through this world and finding healing and new perspectives for areas of life where we've lost hope.

Audrey Velez, creative producer at Willow Creek Community Church and conference manager at The Justice Conference

How to Fix a Broken Record

How to Fix a Broken Record

Thoughts on Vinyl Records, Awkward Relationships, and Learning to Be Myself

Amena Brown

 ZONDERVAN®

ZONDERVAN

How to Fix a Broken Record
Copyright © 2017 by Amena Brown Owen

Requests for information should be addressed to:
Zondervan, *3900 Sparks Dr. SE, Grand Rapids, Michigan 49546*

ISBN 978-0-310-34933-4 (softcover)

ISBN 978-0-310-35160-3 (audio)

ISBN 978-0-310-34934-1 (ebook)

Scripture quotations are taken from The Holy Bible, New International Version®, NIV®. Copyright © 1973, 1978, 1984, 2011 by Biblica, Inc.® Used by permission of Zondervan. All rights reserved worldwide. www.Zondervan.com. The "NIV" and "New International Version" are trademarks registered in the United States Patent and Trademark Office by Biblica, Inc.®

Published in association with William K. Jensen Literary Agency, 119 Bampton Court, Eugene, Oregon 97404.

Cover design: Curt Diepenhorst
Cover illustration: Swillklitch / iStock
Interior design: Kait Lamphere
Interior imagery: istock.com/AlexandrBognat

First printing September 2017 / Printed in the United States of America

My great-grandmother picked cotton
and worked in a tobacco factory
so my grandmother could work at a hospital
so my mom could become a nurse
so I could become a poet.
May the words I write
and the life I live
make you proud.
May I always walk
with your courage and determination
wrapped around my shoulders.

Contents

Introduction 17

PART ONE:

Love and Be Yourself

1. The Myth of the Cool 23
2. On Having Big Feet. 27
3. Natural Hair. 31
4. My Princess Problem 36

PART TWO:

Dating

5. When Love Was Innocent 45
6. When Love Goes Wrong. 49
7. Late Expectations. 57
8. Dear Mr. Nice Guy 64
9. When Love Goes Good. 68
10. When Waiting Gets Weird 75

PART THREE:

Marriage

11. On Being a Terrible Bride 81
12. Letter to Myself on My Wedding Night 86
13. The Worst Marriage Advice 91
14. Marriage Boot Camp 99
15. Marriage Lessons 103
16. The Mystery of Marriage 106

PART FOUR:

Lessons in Adulting

17. The Power of Yes 113
18. The Power of No 117
19. Reasons Why Social Media Is the Best
    Thing That Ever Happened to Me 121
20. Reasons Why Social Media Is the Worst
    Thing That Ever Happened to Me 126
21. Failure 131
22. Success 134

PART FIVE:

Ctrl+Alt+Surrender

23. Soul and Body 141
24. Needle Point 145
25. In Google We Trust 148
26. Janet Jackson and Control 152
27. Ministry of Disappointment 155

PART SIX:

Home

28. Adventures in Staying 163
29. Family Business 166
30. Warrior Women 169
31. Church 174
32. Roots 181
33. Go Ahead and Get Happy 191

PART SEVEN:

Searching for the Groove

34. Vinyl Destinations 197
35. Finding Your Voice 207
36. God Is in the Groove 213

Liner Notes 217

Introduction

Book introductions are awkward. There's no coffee, no chai, no always-too-small plates filled with mini cheesecakes and key lime pie to juggle while answering questions like "What do you do?" and "Where are you from?" and trying to appear more interested in the conversation than you are that some genius managed to infuse the awesome taste of key lime pie into something as small as a bite-size Snickers.

There is no eavesdropping on other people's conversations. No staring at your phone as you aimlessly scroll social media because you know only two people and one of them went to the bathroom and one of them saw somebody cute across the room and cares more about getting dates than they care about helping you meet people.

We don't have a super-extroverted wing-person to guide us through our first meeting, telling me what's super awesome about you and telling you what's super awesome about me. We just have these pages and the words written here.

So, hi. Thanks for reading this. It's nice to meet you. I'm

originally from San Antonio, Texas, but I live in Atlanta, Georgia. ATL is home. Yes, we say ATL or Atlanta, not Hotlanta, as some random weatherperson would have you believe. I perform spoken word poetry and write books and wear sneakers as much as I possibly can.

Where are you from? What do you do? Tell me a slightly funny story so I can chuckle awkwardly.

If you're hoping to find instructions on fixing a literally broken record, I don't have much to offer.

If you're hoping to find some thoughts here about fixing a figuratively broken record like "seeing someone I think is attractive makes me act unattractively awkward" or "someone told me once I'll never be smart enough to [fill in the blank with your dream here]" and you find yourself leaning against the wall at all the parties refusing to dance, scrolling Facebook and seeing your friends' dreams become reality while you pull your comfort zone up to your neck and criticize them, then we've got a lot to talk about.

The stories here are all true, but some of the names have been changed to protect the innocent and the guilty, and some of the names have been left the same for comedic value. As you and I pull our old records out of the sleeves, as you take a listen to the rhythm of where you are and examine the metronome of the off-kilter beats that led you here, be kind to yourself. Sometimes the things in your past are not kind, and sometimes the way you view yourself or your actions isn't kind either.

You and I will both bring our broken records here, the lies and sentence fragments that shatter growth, progress, loving, and being loved. You and I will discover that we never had the power to fix our broken records in the first place, but there is

Someone who doesn't just fix them; in fact, Jesus heals. God makes beautiful music that he is always recording for you and me, melodies of grace and rhythms of mercy, lyrics that he paints into the smiles of strangers. You have lies you need to give up, and Jesus has everlasting truth to give you.

So put the needle to your record. Put on your headphones. Listen to the rhythm God is putting down, and watch God make whole what's broken.

Part One

Love and Be Yourself

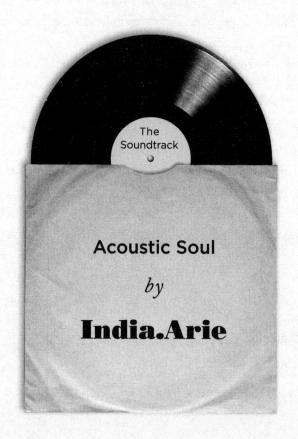

The Soundtrack

Acoustic Soul

by

India.Arie

 There are only a handful of artists I can say I own all their albums, and India.Arie is one of them. Her debut album, *Acoustic Soul*, demonstrated her musicianship, her songwriting, and her determination to be her full and absolute self.

In "Video," India sang so many things we had in common. I don't always shave my legs. I don't always comb my hair. I don't always keep my nail polish fresh. I am also learning to love and be myself. I met her once, right after college when I was working as the assistant to an event producer at a fund-raising gala where she was performing. I was the utmost professional, making sure she had her vegan eats, even if it meant grabbing someone else's limo and hightailing it to the nearest Indian restaurant. After her performance, my boss handed me a Swarovski crystal award to give to India because she knew I was a big fan.

I handed India the award, and she giggled with a smile that rivaled Swarovski's luster. "Oh my gosh! I *love* crystal!" she said.

I knew this was the only fan moment I'd get, so I went for it. "India, I love your music. 'Strength, Courage, and Wisdom' is my *song*! I listen to it sometimes when I'm running on the treadmill." I ran in place, demonstrating how I run when I'm on the treadmill, and proceeded to sing "Strength, Courage, and Wisdom" off-key.

She laughed with me and said thank you, which basically meant we had become best friends forever.

CHAPTER 1

The Myth of the Cool

I was never a cool kid. I spent most of grade school in the library. I wore big-frame glasses. Not the hipster kind that are in style now; I'm talking about the plastic kind of glasses that my mom bought for me because reading the chapter I was currently devouring was way more important to me than remembering not to roll over my glasses while sleeping.

Since my first day of kindergarten, trying to become the one who gets to split the graham crackers down the perforated line, I've been searching for cool. It felt like some exclusive club you had to belong to, a secret society with handshakes, hairstyles, and passwords.

In elementary school, I traded snacks for cool currency. In sixth grade, I tutored junior high football players in spelling, hoping to add points to my cool account.

The transition from elementary school to junior high is pretty significant. In my suburban Maryland school district, we went from putting our snacks in cubbyholes to putting our book bags in lockers and having to remember the lock combination. It was the first time it occurred to me that boys weren't completely gross. It was the year of my first crush, Travis, who looked like a mini Luke Perry from *Beverly Hills 90210* and is probably the reason I never excelled at math. Looking at him in his white T-shirt and jeans was so much more interesting than multiplication.

That was the year big booty Derek asked me when I was gonna let him "hit that," and all I knew was that he was talking about something nasty that I had no intentions of letting him do. It was the year puberty came to visit all of us, the year I went to my first school dance and discovered television didn't lie to us about the boys being on one side of the room and the girls on the other. I wore floral pants and an oversized Gap sweater to that dance. I told my junior high niece about this outfit, and she asked, "What's the Gap?" Sigh.

One afternoon on the way home from school, my classmate Robert pointed out to me and everyone else in the back of the bus that my glasses were dirty. Then he spit on them and told me that should help me clean them. There was no recovering from that. I'm not quick-witted so I spent most of the bus ride home with spit on my glasses, my cheeks hot with embarrassment.

I'm pretty far from junior high now, but I still remember his full name, his hairstyle, the sound of the other kids giggling in the back of the bus, and the immediate feeling that I didn't belong.

In eighth grade, I tried crushing on the coolest, newest guy in school, following behind his kente cloth Cross Colours shorts set on the way to pre-algebra class. In high school, I baked cupcakes for the football players, handing them out with a smile on Fridays before pep rally.

I got such good grades in Algebra II that my best friend, Adrienne, and I received a scholarship to pre-calculus in summer school, and we happily attended. We were a special kind of nerd. During my junior year of high school, I transferred from a small, homogenous private school to a large, diverse public high school. The first day, I wore a flowered dress with tube socks and K-Swiss sneakers. I loved books more than fashion.

As I walked into the cafeteria, I passed all the typical tables: jocks, cheerleaders, pretty girls, the gang affiliated and those who wanted to be, the goth and pierced, the drama club, the weirdos—and then there was my table. We were a mix of nerd with a splash of goody-two-shoes and a whole lot of down-to-earth girl.

One day we all grow up and leave our high school and college lives behind to experience "the real world," but like our younger selves, most of us are still searching for our coveted seat at the cool kids' table. We find ourselves jockeying for position, competing against people we assume, based on their Facebook comments, Twitter posts, or Pinterest pins, must be way cooler than we are.

Cubbyholes are replaced with cubicles; the back of the bus is replaced with social media; and even though we are adults, even though we are no longer trapped in the confines of puberty, we still long to be a cool kid. We still feel like we have something to prove—to ourselves, to our parents, to our ex, to any naysayers. We hope we'll say the right joke in the break room to prove to our coworkers we're cool enough to be accepted. We see an opportunity, but we don't go for it because we are sure someone else is more qualified or more deserving.

I needed that seat at the cool kids' table. I wanted to be invited, validated, and approved of. I wanted someone to tell me I was smart enough, pretty enough, good enough, and cool enough. I wanted to belong. I still do.

Now that I'm far removed from my high school self and have learned that K-Swiss sneakers don't match every outfit, I've discovered the cool kids' table is an illusion. I worked long and hard to be considered popular or acceptable, only to find I would need to work indefinitely to stay in someone else's cool graces or that the only way for me to keep my seat at the table was to try to be anyone except myself.

The cool we've been searching for is all around us, even when we don't recognize it. Our community—the artists, activists, leaders, entrepreneurs, pastors, poets, weirdos, and nerds we have the privilege to call friends; the people who love, challenge, encourage, question, push, and support us—is our cool kids' table.

Maybe instead of trying so hard to impress, flatter, or compete with each other, we should gather a diverse group of people around our dinner or coffee tables. Maybe we should decide that one of the rules for our cool kids' table is that no one gets rejected just because they think, look, or dress differently from us. Maybe the only criteria for our cool kids' table are good conversation and delicious food. There's plenty of love, grace, acceptance, and K-Swiss to go around.

CHAPTER 2

On Having
Big Feet

When my mom took me to my annual doctor appointment when I was eleven, the doctor measured my feet at a women's size seven and a half.

"Your daughter's feet are trying to tell you she is going to be tall," the doctor said.

My mom looked down at my L.A. Gears, knowing time was running short before they'd have to be replaced.

The next year, during my first semester as a sixth grader at Benjamin Banneker Middle School, I rode the bus home for the first time. I surveyed the seats: cool kids in the back, scared kids in the front. I was middle of the road, definitely not cool but not super scared, so I sat about four rows from the back—close enough to hear the jokes the cool kids were saying, far enough away not to be considered one of them.

That day, I caught eyes with an eighth grader whose brown skin and long hair I admired. As soon as we locked eyes in the middle of a great guffaw about something that was wrong with some other kid on the bus, her eyes took me in: glasses, cornrows, matching pants and shirt set, ankle socks, and my fresh-for-the-first-day-of-school Keds. Her eyes landed on my Keds and never returned to my face.

"Look at this one," she said.

All eyes turned to me, and my cheeks hit a heat index of 103.

"What size shoe you wear?" she asked.

This is the equivalent of being at a comedy show on a first date and the comedian asking, "Y'all together?" You know what's coming. You know it's going to be awkward and uncomfortable. But something inside you almost feels like you won something, like (SURPRISE!) you thought this was a comedy show where a comedian was about to ruin this first date's chance of ever becoming a second one, but actually you are the chosen contestant for *The Price Is Right* or *Deal or No Deal* or *How to Be a Millionaire*. So come on down! Spin the wheel! Guess how much this canned good costs! Call a Lifeline! Guess how much money is in this briefcase! You guessed it, a million dollars! You won! Here's money and a car and a year's supply of fabric softener!

Instead, you become a part of the bit. You become a part of the show in a way you didn't want to. You came to the show to laugh and forget about whatever is going wrong in your life. Now you're in a room where you are hearing laughter but not your own, and you are left to smile as if you don't have sweat running out of each of your pores, as if this is your idea of a good time.

So I answered her question, because something in me had to hope she wanted a pair of Keds like mine and wanted to know where my mom had bought them, or that she was dying to tell me how cool I was.

"Eight," I said with a half-smile that I hoped would encourage her to think of a compliment.

"Your feet look like planks," she said and demonstrated from her seat what it must be like to walk on feet as long as mine.

"Yeah, she walking on boats!" another cool kid said, because this is a fairly successful tactic in keeping oneself from being made fun of—join in making fun of someone else in hopes of deflecting the attention from yourself.

They laughed. They made more jokes. I can't even remember what the jokes were. They were still laughing when I got off at my stop and considered my long feet, tall height, and bony legs as if they had betrayed me.

Hurtful words have a weeds-like way of tangling themselves around your image of yourself until the truth of who you are gets choked out by a joke someone told at your expense, by critical words someone said to cover their own insecurity, by mean lies you learn to live with as truth.

I hated being tall. You will not find any childhood pictures of me sneaking into my mom's high heels. I didn't want to be taller. I hated shopping for shoes. By the time I was in high school, my size ten feet were left with the ugly, forsaken comfort shoes on the store rack. It was as if all the ladies who wore size ten went into the store at the same time and ransacked all the cool shoes.

I stayed faithful to rocking fresh sneakers and cute flats because I didn't want to draw more attention to my feet or my height. I wore a pair of shoes until they were threadbare. My best friend, Kimberly, was the first person to teach me that some shoes had a season and were not supposed to be worn year-round. Kimberly loves shoes—heels, boots, sneakers, heels, sandals, heels. She told me how when she went into a department store, the shoes called out to her, and I wondered if they were whispering too quietly because they never called out to me—until I was in my mid-twenties, preparing for a Valentine's Day performance.

The outfit I had planned to wear would not go with sneakers or flats, so I ventured into a department store to see about a red heel—and it happened. What Kimberly said was true. A pair of red heels, shiny with a heel made of cork, called out to me. I tried them on and didn't recognize myself or how I felt.

The salesperson told me there was a buy-one-get-one-half-off sale, and according to the unspoken rules of shopping, one should never buy one pair without buying a subsequent pair for half off. I walked the whole shoe department—kitten heels, orthopedics, wedges, patent leather, grunge boots, snakeskin. Then this pair of stiletto, peep-toe leopard heels said, "Hey girl," so I tried them on. All those years, my height and long feet seemed like things I should hide or compensate for, but in those pumps, my height turned from awkward and gangly to Serena Williams–strong. My plank-long feet turned into elegance made for a slipper better than Cinderella's glass one.

Yes, my feet are long, with no hope of an arch. Yes, in the right scenario, some of my toes could be confused for fingers. But they are mine, and they are the only pair of feet I'll get.

So I'm going to dance with these feet and sometimes paint my fingertoenails. One day I might rock a fresh pair of sneakers, and the next day I might attempt a Beyoncé walk in a pair of stilettos. No matter where my journey leads me, I'm learning to appreciate these feet taking me every step of the way.

CHAPTER 3

Natural Hair

It was 1989. Not Taylor Swift's *1989*, but the actual 1989—the year of Tiffany, Debbie Gibson, the side ponytail, and neon everything. I was getting ready for a friend's birthday party and decided to force my thick, small curls into a side ponytail. There were sore arms and a sore scalp as my hair would not conform. I started to cry in frustration that once again my hair just wouldn't do what Brooke Shields's hair and the hair of my blonde and brunette classmates could do.

It was the first moment I noticed how different it was to be a black girl. It was the first moment I wondered if black girl was what I really wanted to be. My mom found me in tears behind the closed door of the bathroom. I begged her to straighten my hair, but between her work schedule as a single mom and the few-and-far-between hair salons that straightened hair without chemical processing, it didn't seem feasible.

The first time I had my hair straightened, I was living with my grandma for a school year while my mom completed army basic training. My grandma had been going to the same hair stylist for years to have her hair pressed and her grays disguised, so it was my rite of passage to sit in Ms. Martha's coveted chair.

Ms. Martha was old-school; she used an iron comb to straighten and a set of Marcel irons to curl. She used a small oven to heat both irons. The price I paid to have straight hair was having two iron instruments placed close enough to my scalp to straighten my hair from the root. It meant guarding my neck and holding down my ears to protect them from what Ms. Martha referred to as "steam" but what actually felt like fire approaching my skin. When you get your hair straightened this way, you wince and sometimes come away with a small burn or two. But when Ms. Martha would turn the chair around so I could see myself in the mirror, my wide Afro had been transformed to hair that reached my shoulders. I was so proud of it.

A few other black girls in my class came to school with freshly straightened tresses, so I inquired about their hair between games at recess. Perm, they told me. Their moms let them get perms. A perm could straighten my hair without me fearing rain or a humid day. A perm could last six to eight weeks before it had to be touched up, which could save my hardworking mama some time. By the time I was in sixth grade, my mom caved to my requests.

The small coils of curls in my natural hair made my hair seem deceptively short, but the perm brought out the truth. I could have long hair too. This time the heat didn't come from iron instruments; it came from strong chemicals. Sometimes I had a scalp scab or two, but my seemingly unruly curls had been changed into the closest I'd ever get to Tiffany or Brooke Shields or Debbie Gibson.

I wore my perm-straightened hair for twenty years. I wore it long. I wore it short, with layers, and all one length. With big hair-sprayed bangs and gelled-down sideburns in the 1990s, and in a Halle Berry–inspired short cut in the 2000s. I kept my perm through all four years at Spelman College, a historically black, all-female undergraduate institution. While many of my Spelman sisters were becoming enlightened about assimilation and our African roots, and had cut out their perms, gone natural, and grown locs, I was faithful to get my perm retouched every six weeks. I was proud of my sisters and their journey to stay in touch with their roots; I just preferred to read books for my journey and keep my roots straight.

My mom raised my sister and me to do a lot of things ourselves, but hair was not one of them. When it came time for perms or color or anything else that could make your hair fall out, she took us to a professional. So I kept my commitment to this, following various stylists from their basements to high-fashion salons, until I moved into my first apartment and for the first time experienced broke-ness: the tension between my bills and expenses and my income.

I could afford basic living expenses but couldn't indulge in luxuries like getting my hair done. So I let my perm grow out the longest I'd ever let it grow. And I liked the curls I felt like I was meeting for the first time. The only problem was that I was growing my perm out from a short cut, so the back of my hair became an Afro first, while the front still had some straight strands hanging on for dear life. I had done as much as I could do, and now I needed the help of a professional.

I went to a salon and ended up in the chair of Giselle, a beautiful brown woman with regal cheekbones and a smile that calmed my nervousness about the future of my curls. She did a close examination of my hair and gave me my options: I'd either have to get my hair braided or wear some other protective style to grow it out, or I'd have to cut it that day. Braids and I never had a good relationship—my scalp hates them—so I chose the haircut.

By that time, I had grown out my hair about an inch and a half. She cut off the ends where there was still perm, and we decided to dye my hair firecracker red to help me make the transition. When she turned me around to face the mirror, I was greeted by this fantastic head of small red curls, less hair than I'd ever had, and more of my face than I'd ever seen.

Note: if you make drastic changes to your hair, don't do them right before you go to work. Make drastic changes when you have a weekend to be a hermit and consider your decision. I went straight to my call center customer service job, where I was working to help change my broke status. When I got there, my coworker, with whom I chatted between calls, started talking to me without taking a good look at me. When she finally saw my new 'do, she gasped.

"What happened?" she asked.

"I decided to cut my hair," I said.

"But why?" she said.

I didn't know how to answer. I was starting to question everything, starting to feel like that same eight-year-old girl crying behind the closed bathroom door. I called my girlfriends who had gone natural and asked for their advice and pep talks. They told me it would take time to adjust. Adrienne told me to go to YouTube and search "natural hair." I wasn't so sure YouTube was going to help me, but when I woke up at 4:00 a.m. freaking out about what I'd done, I took her advice.

I watched video after video. I learned about the Big Chop—when you cut off your perm and straight hair, and all that's left is a TWA (Teeny Weeny Afro). I learned about sulfate-free shampoos, co-washing, coconut oil, hair masks, two-strand twists, and twist outs. One woman even had a photomontage of her natural hair journey set to Kirk Franklin's "Imagine Me." I may or may not have ugly cried watching that one.

My hair was telling me something about who I was. My hair was showing me what it really meant to love myself. When Jesus says, "Love your neighbor as yourself," he's telling you to do two things: love your neighbor *and* love yourself. Staring at my natural hair the first few months brought back all the negative things I had ever felt or been told about my hair, brought back all my broken records.

Too nappy. Too big. Too thick. Too kinky. Too difficult. Too rough. Too much.

For me, this journey meant that if I was truly going to love myself, I had to learn to love my hair too. I had to accept that God didn't make any mistakes when he made my hair to curl up in the rain or to stand up and out. The God who created the universe, made the leaves, and fashioned the trees also uniquely designed my hair. And if I was going to love others well, I better also learn to love myself and how God made me.

We all have something about the way God has made us that we have been taught or trained, consciously and subconsciously, not to love. It may not be your hair or height. It may be your freckles, your curves, your nose, or the size of your earlobes. It may be the color of your skin or if you have fingertoes. As we learn to love ourselves and how God uniquely made us, we can better love other people and see in them reflections of the amazing image of God.

CHAPTER 4

My Princess Problem

I stood in front of a room filled with young girls and women, first graders to college students. I had been asked to speak about words they should always carry with them. Being in a room with girls and women younger than me always brings up my own journey from girl to woman. What were things I wish had been said to me? What were the words spoken to me that wounded me, that I had to unlearn later?

"Who is your favorite Disney princess?" one of the girls asked.

"I don't have a favorite Disney princess," I said.

The entire room gasped.

How could I explain my troubled princess history? How should I define the complications behind my princess complex to the young faces in front of me?

I cycled through all the Disney movies I knew, the classic Disney films I'd grown up with before there was *Frozen* and

Brave. I thought of *Snow White*, *Cinderella*, and *Sleeping Beauty*, how I never identified with their fair skin and straight hair. I recalled father-daughter dialogue from every heartfelt movie I'd ever seen. Unlike these movie-scene daughters, I had never been called daddy's princess.

I grew up with cordially divorced parents. There was no ugly custody battle, no fights and arguments in my presence. They decided their marriage wouldn't survive, but they both loved me and would keep their respect for each other as they worked together to raise me. I lived with my mom, and toward the end of elementary school, when my dad remarried and returned to the States from his military travels, I went to visit him, my new stepmom, and my new sister and brothers during the summer.

As we navigated the growing pains of a newly blended family, there was no time taken for porch soliloquies about "being daddy's princess" or going on father-daughter dates. I had grown too old to sit on my dad's lap or learn to dance with my feet on top of his. We were all traversing the awkward terrain of what happens when one family breaks and a second family gets created, while each of us tried to survive, to find a way to put ourselves back together.

In my mind, princesses were girls who wore tiaras and bouffant dresses. They were girls who blushed through daddy speeches about how special and beautiful they are, that no matter how old they got or how tall they grew, they would always be daddy's princess. They were girls who had fairy godmothers, spells, flawless cartoon makeup, and perfect hair.

When I visited my friends' homes in elementary school and watched their dads dote over them, I realized the princess life I had imagined was a real-life experience for some of them. After school, they came home to a mommy and daddy. These girls were daddy's princesses, and maybe one day, Prince Charmings would ask for their hands in marriage and make them queens.

I spent my summers getting reacquainted with my dad, stepmom, and siblings and hoping they were also getting to know me as I changed and grew up. I sang choir music in the car with my stepmom and talked with my dad about what I learned in woodshop (a class I took chiefly so I could discuss it with him). I watched wrestling and *Family Guy* with my brothers and talked hip-hop with them until way past midnight. We played Spades and ate steak and fried chicken. We sang and played instruments for my grandmother, who always expected a performance when the whole family was together. Here, there were no princes, no princesses, no royal courts, no magic, no spells—just the imperfect ways we all tried to love and know each other.

When I returned home, my mom's house was not a place born of fairy tales either. Our household was helmed by my mom and grandma, two strong women who could not wait on Prince Charming to rescue them and so became "can-do" women instead. They taught my sister and me to be the same.

My grandma was Wonder Woman, refusing to fit into the narrow category people drew for her because she was black, because she was a woman, because she was a widow raising four kids. She fought, worked hard, walked quickly, wore pants when her church denomination said women weren't allowed to, and taught me how to play "He Is Lord" on the piano.

Life required too many doors to be kicked down for my mom to don Cinderella's glass slippers or wait for the magic wand of a fairy godmother. I grew up in a house of *super-sheroes*. Mom was my real-life version of Storm from the *X-Men*. She may not have been able to control the weather, but she didn't let the circumstances of life dictate who or what she had to be. In the years she raised me, my mom wore clogs as a neonatal nurse, combat boots as an army soldier, flats as a class instructor, and Mary Janes as a hospital liaison.

I wasn't raised to be a damsel in distress, to be a woman who waits for life to happen to her, so I never dressed up as a princess, never imagined myself wearing a tiara, and preferred a fresh pair of sneakers in case I needed to walk quickly, run, or dance. I found my fairy tales and sheroes in Toni Morrison's *The Bluest Eye*, Maya Angelou's poem "Phenomenal Woman," Lauryn Hill's album *The Miseducation of Lauryn Hill*, Alice Walker's *The Color Purple*, and John Steptoe's *Mufaro's Beautiful Daughters*.

Later in life, I realized I had a lot more in common with Disney and fairy-tale princesses than I thought. Most of them didn't grow up in a traditional family. Many of them grew up without their mothers or fathers due to death, war, work, or abandonment. The absence of their parent led them to heartbreak and hard times and left them at the mercy of wicked witches, mean villains, and cruel stepmothers. In a fairy tale, the interruption caused by a break in the family is part of what propels the protagonist to realize she is a princess or that she can become one.

I talked about the princess problem with another room of young women—teen girls who had lived enough hard life to be twice their age. They were a part of the girls' residential program at Wellspring Living, an organization that serves survivors of trafficking, commercial sexual exploitation, and abuse. As these brave young women were beginning recovery, I sat at a table with them once a month or so, and we wrote together.

We wrote about God, about the past, about things we love,

about wounds. I asked them to write about what they thought about the word *princess*. I was curious to see if they had the same complicated relationship I had with this word. Some found it easy to identify with fairy tales; some, like me, couldn't bring themselves to believe in fairy tales based on the harsh realities they had experienced.

We tried an experiment. I asked them to invent their own princess and kingdom. We used our pens to describe what our version of a princess would be like, what the rules of our kingdom would be, how we would treat the people who lived there.

We wrote about how they would help those who lived in their kingdom. Princess fashions ranged from gold to couture to sneakers and jeans. As we read aloud our various inventions of princess, I realized there was power in the exercise. Movies, magazines, fairy tales, or comic books don't have to be the only things that define girlhood and womanhood for my generation or any of the generations of girls to follow. We get to tell our own stories.

I'm learning I don't have to be a fragile princess or a super-shero with no weaknesses. I am somewhere in between. I am human. I am a woman. Sometimes I fight. Sometimes I win. Sometimes I need to be rescued. Sometimes I look at myself in the mirror and actually think the woman looking back at me is beautiful. Some days I struggle to believe that's true, even though the fact that God made me and each of us beautiful doesn't change based on how we feel. I fail; I make mistakes. I need love, care, concern. I am strong, and I am weak.

I hope to say to young girls what I continue to say to my little girl self: You can be your own version of a Disney princess or a comic book shero. Be unique. Be different. Be weird. Be a nerd. Whether you wear a tutu or Chucks, have freckles or rock an Afro, are shy and soft-spoken or bold and blunt, be yourself.

God doesn't write fairy tales, but he is always writing a good story. He's taking your best and your worst moments and incorporating them into the story he was writing for you before you were born.

It's easier to be a princess in the pages of a book or in the scene of a movie. In real life, there are no convenient plot devices, no villains to scapegoat, and often no neatly written happy endings.

In the story God is writing in my life, I am learning to love my version of princess, even if it means no princess at all. Most important, I am learning that God's story has a hero who knows no kryptonite, a father who never leaves his children, and a love that doesn't depend on perfection, a fairy godmother, a certain level of income or background or skin tone, a Prince Charming, or superpowers. God's story is about grace, adventure, peace, risk, courage, and trust, and that story is the best page-turner of them all.

Part Two

Dating

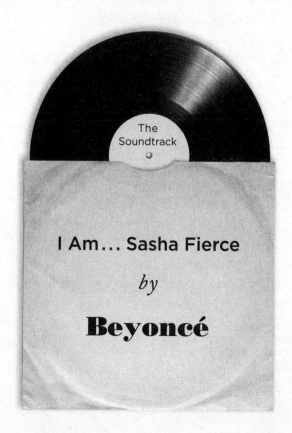

The Soundtrack

I Am... Sasha Fierce

by

Beyoncé

This album is pretty indicative of my dating life: full of love, infatuation, heartbreak, and daydreaming about what I would do if I were a boy. With this album, Beyoncé is responsible for the phrase "put a ring on it" becoming a part of our lexicon. "Single Ladies (Put a Ring on It)" made the bouquet toss at a wedding less awkward when I was single. When I heard that staccato drumbeat, I stood up and strutted my stuff before I realized it was all a wedding trick for some new bride to send the ladies who were left single into a deep depression if we didn't catch the bouquet.

Beyoncé taught me that being a hustler wasn't just for wannabe gangsters. Being a hustler was for divas, for women who eat donuts like a boss, who will not accept "no dessert" for an answer. Okay, Beyoncé didn't exactly say these things, but I'm pretty sure underneath all the lyrics that is what she meant.

CHAPTER 5

When Love
Was Innocent

I went on one date in high school. My mom and grandma allowed this mostly because the date took place after I graduated. I was already eighteen years old, and the gentleman in question had been offered scholarships and acceptance to all the branches of military academies in the country. My grandma actually highlighted his name in my high school graduation program and questioned why I hadn't thought about dating him before now.

He was sweet, chivalrous, nerdy, and kind, the best combination for my first date ever. It was the late 1990s, and most of the guys I had crushes on in high school were pretending to be the gangsta they thought they saw in Snoop Dogg or Dr. Dre. My first date was a cute nerd I'd always wanted to know more about as I sat near him in AP English class.

During the last few days of our last year of high school, my classmates and I were all swapping yearbooks, mostly signing things we didn't mean or things we'd regret later. "Have a great summer" wouldn't suffice when we'd already seen our last high school summer by then. So "have a great summer" turned into "have a great life!" and "K.I.T." and "don't forget about me."

Within six months' time, we would forget about most of those people and would keep in touch with only a handful. Something inside me knew this, so I started getting a bit more cavalier with the messages I wrote in people's yearbooks. If I didn't care for them, I kept it short and sweet, and if I thought they were cool, I said so, even if I'd never said so before. So when the nerdy guy and I exchanged yearbooks, I went for it. I wrote that I'd always thought he was cute and smart, signed my name quickly, and closed his yearbook, thinking he wouldn't read it until after neither of us could do anything about it. He read it right away and smiled. This made me smile too.

We danced together to an Usher song at our senior party the night of graduation, and he asked for my number and said he wanted to take me out sometime. I felt like I was starring in my own chick flick. No guy had ever said the words "take you out sometime" to me. It sounded so adult, so fancy. It sounded like a romantic dinner and candlelight and walking through the autumn leaves in Central Park. I didn't care that San Antonio didn't have fall leaves or that I'd never even been to Central Park. My life had just gotten amazing!

It took him a few days (*agonizing* days to my eighteen-year-old self, let's be honest!), but he finally called, and we scheduled our first date. He said he could pick me up at 3:00 p.m., and my mom said I had to be home by 10:00 p.m. This was longer than she allowed me out on the night of my senior prom. My grandma and seven-year-old sister stood at the door smiling at and eyeing him when he arrived. We got into his car—no parents, no chaperones, just us. We went to the movies and then went to play pool. I pretended I didn't know a thing about pool so he could put his arms around me. And then we went to Sonic. I ordered a milkshake, and he ordered a slush, and then we tasted each other's drinks, which was the equivalent of a kiss to me.

We talked about our futures and how we wished we had talked more all those months we sat near each other in AP English class. He told me how he was excited and nervous about attending a military academy. I told him how I was excited and nervous about going to Spelman and being so far away from home. We had so much hope and life ahead of us.

He brought me home before curfew (bonus points from Mom!) and walked me inside so Mom would know I was home safe. After appropriately timed family greetings, I walked him out to the porch. We hugged, and then he told me he was moving away in two weeks. Such was life in a town full of military families. Not only was his summer going to be cut short because the military academy required cadets to start their first year of college a month earlier than most schools, but his dad had been assigned a new duty station, and the whole family was moving to Oklahoma.

We had just discovered that two nerdy brown kids in AP English class had more to talk about than Shakespeare, but we would never get the chance for a second date. We kissed each other on the cheeks and hugged each other for all the past and future time we knew we'd miss.

We promised to write each other. He was one of the first people I wrote to from my brand-new college email address when I was still trying to figure out exactly how email worked. We emailed about our experiences voting in our first presidential election, about the rigor of college classes. We kept in touch for years, and even now that both of us are married and he has become a dad, it's wonderful to see him doing so well.

My first date taught me romance didn't have to be the danger zone I'd been told to avoid. It could be hopeful and full of possibility. It could be kisses on the porch and Sonic drinks in the summer. It could be beautiful and innocent, and I tried really hard to continue to believe this, even after heartbreak taught me love could be disappointing with the same force that it could be blissful.

CHAPTER 6

When Love Goes Wrong

Growing up in church youth group and college campus ministry in the era of *I Kissed Dating Goodbye* and "I waited until I got married to have my first kiss" meant I could count on one hand the number of dates I went on between eighteen and twenty-five years old.

I went to college, and despite my all-female school being right across the street from the all-male Morehouse College and coed Clark Atlanta University, I put a personal ban on dating then. It wasn't that I felt dating was morally wrong. Many times I wanted to jump out and grab the nearest set of male pectorals and sexy shoulders that walked past me. I didn't date because I was scared.

The church I grew up in and my hardworking single mama had supported me so much and in so many ways on my journey to college. My biggest fear was returning home carrying not only a pregnant belly but also my and their dashed hopes and dreams.

So I had a few crushes, but I avoided dating and instead buried my head in my books and in my local campus ministry.

When I graduated from college, I immersed myself in college ministry at my church. I was comfortable around guys as long as we were friends or working together on something. When I turned twenty-five, I realized it had been seven years since I'd sat across the table from a man I found attractive on anything that resembled a date.

So I left my church bubble, started meeting guys, and started dating. I dated good guys, trifling guys, church guys, shy guys, older guys, and younger guys. Then I met Coen. I saw him leaning against a wall at an arts event, as if his lean was holding the whole party together. We introduced ourselves and told the kind of jokes you tell when you're hoping to get the other person's phone number.

We talked on the phone. We saw each other out at more events. We met up for dinner and talked until the restaurant closed. We left the restaurant and talked on the phone too late for two people who had to get up for work in the morning. I told him I was a virgin and that I intended to wait to have sex until I got married. At the time, I thought announcing to men that I was a virgin would help me figure out those who were committed to abstinence and those who weren't. I learned later this announcement did nothing but encourage some of the guys I dated to see if they could swindle me out of my drawers. An announcement I thought would be a deterrent for men determined to have sex with any woman they were dating became an unintended bull's-eye.

Coen found my stance curious, especially at my age. He asked me things like, "What if you get married and the sex is bad?" and "Does this make you a prude?"

"Do you believe sex is a gift like singing?" I asked. "Like some people are born with the ability to do it well and some people aren't?"

"No, it takes practice. You learn how to do it better the more sex you have," he said.

"So two people could get married, practice sex with each other, and learn how to do it well for the rest of their lives, right?" I said.

"Yeah, I guess so," he said.

That night on the phone he told me, "Don't like me. This isn't going to work. You're a virgin, and I'm a fornicator. Those two don't mix."

I believed him, so we both put each other in the friend zone. Sometimes this is not a "love you like a brother or sister" zone. Sometimes the friend zone is a place you put attractive people whom you wish you could date but for whatever reason can't. We existed for years in each other's friend zones while constantly flirting with the idea of what it would be like if that friend zone didn't exist.

Coen was a churchgoing, successful, full-time artist. We were in each other's friend zones long enough to see a few relationships in both of our lives come and go. I'd always hoped one of those times we both found ourselves single that maybe we'd give dating each other a try.

One day when my car wouldn't start on the way to my corporate job, I called him to jump my car, because with his full-time artist schedule he was the only person I knew who wasn't already at an office job for the day. After my car cranked up and all the jumper cables were put away, he said, "You owe me for this."

"What do I owe you?" I said.

"How about dinner?" he said.

"I could do that."

I made spaghetti. We talked that night about life, about love. We talked about our friendship and why all this time it had remained only a friendship when our original intent was to be more than friends. We kissed . . . the kind of kiss that made us discover no amount of pretending to be friends could hide the chemistry building between us.

He was honest with me. He'd never dated a woman he didn't have sex with, but he was open to trying to date without it. We decided to give dating a try. We went out to dinner. We literally watched Netflix and chilled before "Netflix and chill" became code for sex. We talked about music, art, film. We debated the merits of poetry and the roles of men and women in relationships.

A few months later, he sent me a text. We should grab dinner, he said. We need to talk, he said. I suspected this did not mean I was going to arrive to dinner to find my family there as he proposed to me.

We sat across the table from each other. We ordered food. I now know this was a terrible idea, because who wants to eat food when you are getting dumped before the bread arrives? After the waiter cleared the menus, Coen looked at me—not in the way he had on other dates when we were having fun or when the chemistry between us swelled to a beautiful crescendo that seemed like it could transform into a love song; he looked at me like he felt sorry for me and for what he was about to say.

"I've reached the end of my celibacy road," he said.

He spoke these words as if he were rescuing me, as if he had pulled me in on a fishing hook and was throwing me back into the sea.

I, however, had not reached the end of my celibacy road. The beginning of my noncelibate road was still obviously a long way off. I was a twenty-eight-year-old virgin, and the man I was falling for was ending our dating relationship because I wouldn't have sex with him. This man I had such great feelings for, the man I foolishly or hopelessly wanted some sort of future with, even if it was only a very immediate future, was taking my heart and puncturing it before our dinner orders arrived.

I didn't know what else to do but be cordial. After dinner, he walked me to my car. He hugged me and said words like "didn't mean to hurt you" and "wish you the best" and that he wanted good things for me. But to me they all sounded like, "You aren't enough. You'll never be enough."

I spent the next few days between anger, hurt, disappointment, and large slices of pie à la mode. I wore sweatpants. I cried. I hoped he would change his mind. I hoped a few times I would change my mind. I tossed around the commitment I'd made to waiting until I got married to have sex and wondered if it was really worth it. I wondered if I was losing the only love I'd ever know over something that sometimes seemed like a technicality and other times seemed like an imperative.

I prayed and I cried. I ate, and sometimes my heart hurt so much I couldn't eat. I wanted so much to give up on the possibility of love. I wondered if my commitment to waiting to have sex until I got married would keep me from the very thing I hoped it would help me get to: marriage.

A couple of months later, I was performing poetry at a women's leadership session where Jeanne Stevens was speaking. She talked about how women assume that in order to lead they should separate their heart, emotions, and feelings from the leadership process. She said every leader should lead with love, and we should ask ourselves, "When do I find myself not leading with love?"

Not only was I still trying to heal the wounds of a broken heart, but the dream career I was trying to build also was looking more like shambles than a solid foundation. I went back to the hotel room that night, where I couldn't sleep for thinking of all the bills I'd have waiting for me back home—bills that added up to a sum that superseded my income.

I thought about love and how, based on my recent experience, love only resulted in wounds. What did I know about love? Isn't this what the story of so many older women in my life had taught me? That love will feel good for a short time, performing some voodoo anesthetic on you, only to sneak up on you with a stabbing pain that will take your breath and your hope away? I'd always thought of love as a dangerous storm where you prepare for how it may destroy you, not a thing you could make a home out of.

I realized I couldn't keep thinking of love like that. I was almost right. Love is a lot like rain. When it's dangerous, it can destroy things. But when it's right, it can make everything around it grow. I didn't want to stop growing because I was so busy preparing for the storm and not seeing the goodness in the rain. Romantic love is a powerful force that can overtake reason, logic, and emotions, but it doesn't have to be something to fear or flinch in front of in preparation for a hit.

I realized I hadn't let my heart fully feel anything about Coen, that even in my personal life I needed to learn to lead with love. The next day on the plane ride home, I listened to Beyoncé's newly released *I Am . . . Sasha Fierce* album, and as she sang her love songs, I realized I was in love with Coen. I'd been in love with him for so long and been unable to admit it. So I typed a letter, and a couple of days later, I put that letter in an email and clicked send.

hey coen,

for some reason, it is much harder for me to write how i feel than say it, but i figured it might be good if i can get this stuff down on a page and send it to you. here goes . . .

i'm in love with you. was probably in love with you when i was dating you but never wanted to say it for fear of letting those emotions run free only for things to come to an end.

for the past couple of days, i've been sitting with that. smiling some and finally not trying to control or quickly get rid of those feelings. then yesterday, underneath all those good feelings arrived some sadness.

after i went through my day, piddled around and did all i had to do, i sat alone in my apartment and started to cry. since we stopped dating i've been focusing so much on trying so hard not to have feelings for you that i missed the whole point.

the point is not to be without feelings; the point is what i do with or about them. i realized that i have to simultaneously love you and let you go.

I excerpted this letter for length, because when you realize you are falling in love, you actually want to take R&B singer Aaliyah's advice and send a four-page letter. You go on and on about every moment of indecision you've ever had about the relationship, every warm, fuzzy, lovey-dovey feeling you've ever had, and then because you're in love, you write more words, feelings, feelings, words, emotions, words, feelings.

I felt like Helen Hunt in my own weird version of *As Good as It Gets*, shuffling through my feelings the way she read that heartfelt but awkward letter to Jack Nicholson's character, but minus the rain that always seems to happen in romantic films during scenes like this, and minus the wet shirt and falling in love with a rude, yet generous curmudgeon.

After Coen read the letter, we talked. It meant a lot to him that I sent him the letter—but it meant the most to me. I hoped Coen would turn to me and tell me I made him want to be a better man. I hoped my love would change him. I learned that love can't change someone into something I want them to be.

The letter didn't change the fact that Coen and I didn't have a future together. It didn't magically make him the best choice for me, or change the reasons we couldn't have a healthy relationship. But the letter showed me I could love. That it was possible for me to let my guard down and love. I realized the lie I'd believed about myself for so long wasn't true. Not only could I love someone, but something about that letter also gave me hope that even though it wouldn't be Coen, I could be loved in return.

CHAPTER 7

Late Expectations

Adrienne and I had saved up enough money to make a trip to New York to (1) celebrate our thirtieth birthdays, (2) lament our singleness, (3) go to Times Square because we thought it would be a difficult place to be depressed, (4) all of the above. But before I get to that, I need to cover some backstory. The backstory is never as important as the front story, but the backstory can provide some context for the front story. And sometimes, as a bonus, it can provide a very entertaining side story.

Here are eight important things that happened prior to my thirtieth birthday:

1. I spent my twenty-ninth birthday training to work as a customer service representative for a cell phone company. Everyone there was broke, including me, so my coworkers put their pennies together and bought me a two-pack of Hostess cupcakes from the vending machine and stuck

coffee stirrers in them, because if we couldn't afford birthday cake, we definitely couldn't afford candles or a lighter.

2. I had a lot of dysfunctional conversations with single guys and went on *a lot* of bad dates, a few of which I will chronicle here:

Dysfunctional telephone conversation with Car Wash Guy

> **Him:** I just found out I have to move to New York.
> **Me:** Oh, cool! New York is a great town.
> **Him:** Yeah, I just don't know what's gonna happen to *us*.
> **My internal thoughts:** *We haven't been on a date yet.*
> *There's an* us?
> **Me:** Well, it sounds like a great opportunity, so I think
> you should go for it.
> **Him:** But then, when will I have my way with you?
> **Me:** How long were you expecting it would take you to
> have your way with me?
> **Him:** About three weeks.
> **My cell phone:** Either you hang up, or I will.

Bad date with Mr. Lavender Pants (who was named this for wearing lavender pants with uncle sandals to our third and last date)

> **Him:** How old are you?
> **Me:** Twenty-seven.
> **Him:** Oh, and you don't have children?
> **Me:** Nope.
> **Him:** Aren't you worried about your uterus?

Dysfunctional telephone conversation with Mr. Control Freak

My clock: 9:30 p.m.

Him: Wanna come over?

Me: No.

Him: Oh, that's right, you're celibate. Me too. I just decided to be celibate. You should come over.

My clock: I can't take this anymore. You know what time it is.

I hope you can discern from this how my dating life was going.

3. I fell in love. Hard. With someone I could never sustain a relationship with. (See previous chapter, "When Love Goes Wrong.")

4. The good guy who got away returned. He was still amazing. I had matured from the girl who breaks up with a guy right after he buys her an expensive dinner, the girl whose main reason for ending said relationship was because he felt too safe (also known as boring, before you've had some therapy) to a girl who could recognize a good man when she saw one. Just as I was thinking we'd rekindle things, he fell in love with someone else and married her. And after the way I'd treated him, I was sure I deserved that snub. (See next chapter, "Dear Mr. Nice Guy.")

5. My best guy friend (and secret crush) from high school showed back up in my life, and we were "talking," meaning spending lots of time on the phone possibly saying words we

didn't mean, but the dream of the words was so beautiful that we kept going with that dream longer than we should have.

6. I got into debt and went broke. I almost lost my car and my apartment. I wasn't sure if I'd ever have a career as a poet, writer, or customer service rep.

7. I grew out my perm, cut my hair, and went natural. Or "did the big chop," as the natural hair ladies say on YouTube. (Read Chapter 3, "Natural Hair.")

8. I finally surrendered. A woman can only take disappointment so many times before she decides the way her life is going is a strong indicator that she's not the best at planning her life and maybe she should leave the planning to God. I'm not sure if you knew this about God, but God manages to have all of time in his hands and handles it pretty well because he's not a human being. I gave up dating the same problematic guy. I surrendered my dreams of having a career as a writer and artist. I hit a really low point. And God resurrected what I surely thought could never come back to life.

I went through a lot, which is why I think it snuck up on me that I was turning thirty. I had so many expectations about what I'd be doing by the time I turned thirty. I imagined I'd be married to a man who was a combination of Idris Elba and Malcolm Gladwell. And we would have these curly-headed kids who spoke in English accents but could quickly change their voices to sound like they were from Baltimore or Brooklyn. And they would be so smart they would only need to be homeschooled for two years because they would put in their entire ten thousand hours before they hit second grade. And we'd spend the rest of our lives traveling around the world between movie sets and speaking engagements as a family.

Instead, I spent the months leading up to my thirtieth birthday digging myself out of debt, mending my broken heart, and accepting that my next decade of life was about to look really different from what I expected. Sometimes my worst broken records are tangled in a false sense of expectations. A lot of times, I'm holding myself to a Facebook standard of living, where everything good must be an announcement with proper filter and graphic design. Where one must move on quickly from one phase of life to the next and follow arbitrary age requirements for one's uterus, as if my Fallopian tubes aren't under enough pressure.

Our trip to New York was a welcome break from the stress. Adrienne and I stayed in a quaint bed-and-breakfast, but from the outside, it looked like an average brownstone. We felt like New Yawkers.

We stood in line to get free entry into the Museum of Modern Art. Adrienne found me crying in front of a Van Gogh and probably regretted agreeing to go on this trip with me for at least two minutes that day.

I'd never seen *A Starry Night* in person, only the tiny graphic in a school textbook. Seeing it in person devastated me in the best way. It was like New York was trying to tell me something. Trying to tell me she wasn't just bright lights and big city. She was more than Times Square and Big Apple trinkets. She was trying to teach me to open my eyes wider, to dream bigger. To not live based on societal expectations but to let myself get so close to the beauty in life that it could devastate and change me. To cry whenever and just because.

We went to see *Fela!* on Broadway, a stage play about Nigerian musician and activist Fela Kuti. Seeing the women's Afros and braided hairstyles on stage made me proud of my decision to cut my hair. Fela's story inspired me. He used his music to fight against oppression in his native Nigeria. He traveled to Los Angeles and New York, and although these cities and their country could never truly be his home, he realized he could take the things he was learning there to help his people be free. I realized maybe I could too.

Adrienne and I ate some of the best pasta I've had in my life at a small, family-owned Italian restaurant just big enough for a farm table to fit inside. We ate Junior's cheesecake in honor of Sean "Puffy" Combs and Da Band, who walked miles for that coveted slice.

We lamented where our present lives had failed to meet our expectations. We were entering our thirties, a time we thought would have included a spouse and possibly children. Neither of us had a boyfriend or a first date on the horizon. As we walked through the West Village eyeing which sneakers to buy, we decided we wouldn't let our circumstances dictate to us the kind of life we'd choose to live. Maybe we weren't married or dating anyone, and maybe we would never get married, but we weren't going to live like we were constantly holding our breath or waiting for life to happen.

We made a promise to each other. We were going to do what God called us to do. We were going to travel and pursue our dreams. We were going to live life to the fullest, even if we became nuns—which, based on our tumbleweed dating lives and nonexistent sex lives, is where we might be headed.

We carried a certain lament with us, but we left New York holding more joy, more hope—not for some Prince Charming to rescue us from our single-girl plight, but more hope in the God who called us and more belief in the women he'd created us to be. We stopped waiting at life's bus stop for some adventure to pick us up. New York taught us that we could walk, drive, and fly to our own adventures.

CHAPTER 8

Dear
Mr. Nice Guy

Dear Mr. Nice Guy,

Good men are hard to find and even harder to keep. It's unforgiveable to let one go. Just like you, they keep slipping through my hands like so much sand in an hourglass. You're right. You are underappreciated. You've been given a bad rap, and truthfully, I preferred a broken and bruised heart to your respectful ways. I'm sorry I said you were boring. I'm sorry I said you were soft. I'm sorry I said you weren't sexy enough. I'm sorry for not giving you a chance.

When we first met, you confused me. Seriously, who's honest anymore, Mr. Nice Guy? Who says what they mean in the dating game these days? I suppose you do, and it's clear you don't believe in playing with my emotions. What's a single woman to do with all that free time, now that there's no reason to spend time psychoanalyzing too-short text messages, missed calls with no voice mail, and first dates that never make it to a second one?

And another thing, Mr. Nice Guy, how dare you be into commitment? I mean, who's into getting serious? Who wants the pressure of a man who wants to be with only me? I much prefer a man who's juggling me and sixty other women across the city. I like a man who keeps me guessing.

Marriage, commitment, rings, his and hers sinks and towels, matching outfits—these words didn't scare you. In fact, you welcomed them, wanted them, wanted me. But I wasn't ready for you. My early-twenties mind couldn't fathom giving up the freedom of singleness to settle down with you. I couldn't bring myself to give up the lottery-like possibility of finding five other men who might be the one. I was standing on the side of the road with a hitchhiker's thumb, passing up the safest ride home. I was waiting for something better. Like baiting a unicorn on a fishing pole, I was stupid to throw you back into the sea that is supposedly running aplenty with fish.

Trust me. When my nights get lonely, when I'm out with some ignorant fool who doesn't know opening the door for a lady from throwing a shot of tequila down his throat, who assumes that dinner and a second date mean sex, I think of you. Don't tell anyone I'm writing this, but sometimes I daydream of you. You, the one any woman would want to bring home to meet a dysfunctional family. You, who would rub my back while my family argues the merit of Scripture and Scrabble, and who would gaze at me with the look that said you loved and accepted me just for me and would do the same for them. You, who would have made love, made babies, and stuck around to deal with me, my horrible hormonal attitude, and alien cravings; stuck around for baby names, birth, pre-K, middle school, college, and empty nest until it was back to just us. You, who, even as you are reading this, forgives the silly me that sent you on your way in the first place.

The phrase "no more Mr. Nice Guy" has haunted me since I ended things with you. You made me question my definition of a man. As if the paramount of testosterone has to equal hairy machismo, never-ending noncommitment, and grunts-only communication. You had character, endurance, perseverance, respect, patience. I was just too fireworks-driven to see it.

You have no reason to trust these words coming from the pen of a woman who so quickly and easily dismissed you, but years and life and trouble and struggle have shaped this woman with the same indelible imprint with which quick rivers create slowly hewn canyons. I see you more clearly now, as I see myself.

I really just wanted to let you know that the phrase "nice guys finish last" is propaganda pushed by bad boys in gentlemen's clothing. Whatever you do in life, don't shy away from being the nice guy, especially not because of women like me. Sooner or later, some woman is going to relish your gentlemanly gestures. She will find your respectful hand in the small of her back so much sexier than a strange first-date hand attempting the squeeze on her inner thigh. She will be swept away by your chivalrous door opening, your coat holding, your gentlemanly chair pulling, and she will not ditch you for the next smooth-swagger, emotionally unavailable slick talker. Hold out for her, and don't settle for less.

Don't worry, you don't have to reply. I wouldn't dare ask you for a second chance. I just wanted to clear the air and hopefully give myself a clean slate. And maybe, just maybe, I'll cross paths with another nice guy. This time I won't give him back.

Sincerely,

Me

CHAPTER 9

When Love Goes Good

After Adrienne and I returned from New York and my last-ditch efforts at dating failed, I decided to try Dr. Henry Cloud's dating program from his book *How to Get a Date Worth Keeping*. Every man I'd ever loved, liked, or had a crush on was now married, in a serious relationship, or otherwise emotionally unavailable. In fact, I'd made an unfortunate hobby of dating men who were emotionally unavailable. In a sea of men, I would always pick out the one who was attractive, funny, smart, and completely unavailable for commitment. When I didn't pick that guy, I was the unavailable one to the kind, chivalrous guy.

My dating life needed fixing, and since Dr. Cloud's book promised it could at least get my dating life healthy, I tried it out with the accountability of my small group from church. They probably thought I was crazy, but they didn't judge me, and they prayed for and with me each step along the way.

The first step was assessing how many men I was meeting in

my life. For two weeks I had to keep a log of how many new guys came across my path. This number amounted to two. After the initial two weeks, I had to make it my business to meet at least five new guys every week, with each guy having some way to get in touch with me, which could be email, phone, or social media.

I joined the Atlanta Hiking Club, and I don't even like to go outside. I went to every single mingle I could find. I strolled the aisles of the grocery store. I introduced myself to men at networking events, even though my church upbringing had taught me it was taboo for a woman to take any initiative with a man.

In Dr. Cloud's program, you had to agree to go out with almost anyone once, and if you had a reason to not go out with them, it had to be a substantial one, like disrespect or feeling unsafe, not what kind of work they did or if their front tooth was crooked or if their laugh sounded like they were drowning. This meant I couldn't discriminate as much about the men I introduced myself to. This also meant I learned about myself and my dating expectations.

Ike taught me that I was open to dating men with a stockier build. Nick didn't have the type of look I typically liked, but when he told me about his hike to Machu Picchu, I enjoyed his descriptions of what he was passionate about and that he taught me something in the process. I learned I found intellect attractive.

I went on a salsa dancing double first date with my friend Camille and two guys we met at a church singles event we crashed. That night, the salsa dance instructor's wife went into labor, so our intended salsa lesson turned into an open-floor dance-off, where my date, who couldn't dance to save his life, made up some off-rhythm steps. I was half-horrified and half-admiring of his confidence. He taught me fun isn't always about being great at everything you do.

None of these guys made it past a couple of dates. We soon discovered one or both of us wasn't a match, but they each showed me my expectations of the types of guys I could date had been too narrow and I had been missing out on growing and learning.

Meeting five new guys a week was rigorous, so I sometimes enlisted friends to take the journey with me to an event where neither of us was sure we'd meet anyone. I searched on meetup.com for any social events I could visit and discovered that Atlanta had a local tall people's club. Yes, this is a real thing. And yes, there is an international tall people's club. Women must be five feet ten inches tall and above to join, and men must be six feet two inches tall and above.

Lindsey from my small group fit the height and the single ready-to-mingle profile, so she met me there. I'm not gonna lie, I had some real expectations. I was expecting a room full of Idris Elbas and George Clooneys. Lindsey and I instead were greeted by a room of tall people that more closely resembled the style of dress our elementary school teachers were fond of in the 1980s versus a room of modelesque, beefcake fellas.

A woman walked up and introduced herself as one of the leaders of the local Atlanta chapter.

"I've been reading a book profiling tall people, and it's really enlightening," she said. "Have you ever talked to a shorter person and felt like they couldn't understand you?"

Lindsey and I caught eyes, but the woman continued talking before we could answer.

"Well, this book says it's because the air down there is different and tall people are actually smarter than short people."

Lindsey looked at me with the same fear and pity with which Jim glared at the camera on the TV show *The Office*. My phone buzzed with a text from a deejay friend of mine whose name was Matt (his friends called him Opie). One of his favorite rappers was in town, and I'd told him I'd meet him at the show. I hadn't, of course, disclosed I had to make a stop at the tall people's club because it was Friday and I'd only met two new guys that week. His text let me know he was headed to the venue.

I looked up at Lindsey and said, "I'd quit this whole program for this guy."

"Get your purse," she said. "Let's go!"

We ducked out before a man dressed in white linen who looked like my pre-algebra teacher came up to introduce himself.

"Go meet this guy at the concert and see what happens! And you owe me for tonight," she said and laughed. (Lindsey, I still owe you a proper night out, girl.)

I drove to the concert feeling disappointed and trying to ignore how fast my heart was beating at the thought of meeting Matt. We had met at church and connected on Myspace. Yeah, wow, Myspace. We were going to be hosting an open mic together, and we were building a show combining spoken word and deejaying. When I'm creating, I have to get my insecurities out first, which means while we worked together, we had all sorts of conversations about our lives and the places we'd come from.

We were great friends, purely platonic, who'd never even flirted with each other. But I'd wanted to be more than his friend for a while and didn't know what to do about it or if there was anything I should do. By the time I met him at the concert, I had gathered my cool enough to hide how happy I was to see him.

The show was poorly planned, and the rapper wasn't having a good night. The show went so badly we decided to leave early.

"Hey, remind me to tell you some thoughts I've been having

that might change the show we've been building," I said as we headed out the door.

"Let's get something to eat and talk about it," he said.

We made our way to a late-night spot that served the bomb empanadas. We talked about art and faith and where the two intersect and sometimes seem to be in conflict with each other. I looked across the table at him and thought, *Not only is he handsome, but he's smart and creative and thoughtful.* And I had a crush on him—the kind of crush that wouldn't so easily be stuffed into the Tupperware container I kept in my heart for feelings not quite convenient to deal with or process.

Matt had been married once before, and the marriage went terribly and ended in divorce. During the years of our friendship, I had watched him heal and find his way back to himself and his calling. As his friend, I was happy to see him enjoying life and having hope for the days ahead, but I had no idea what his thoughts were about his romantic future.

He kept going on for months about how he had to get his ducks in a row before he could see himself in a relationship. I wasn't sure what those ducks were or how many of them he had to get in a row. I mainly wanted to know how many ducks had to stand in a perfect line before we could go on a dinner date. I sensed many of those ducks were financial. He had a certain lifestyle he felt he had to live to have a woman in his life. I respected that, but I didn't need a man to be in a certain tax bracket or drive a certain car to date me. I needed to know he loved Jesus, walked in his calling, had fun, was comfortable in his skin, and had room in his own soul to give me space to be myself and fly.

So I did the only thing I knew to do. I asked him questions like a journalist. I had two in mind.

"If you had all your ducks in a row, would you date?" I asked.

"Yeah, I'd date," he said.

"Do you have hope that God has somebody out there for you?" I asked.

He paused. And got silent. Really silent. So silent I almost regretted asking the question. But I needed the answer so badly that I refused to let the awkward silence dissuade me. I was determined to sit there awkwardly until he answered. I figured his answer would tell me whether we were destined for the friend zone or if there was more potential for our connection to each other.

"Yeah, I have hope," he said. "I think I have some fears. Some of those are healthy fears, and some are unhealthy fears. My healthy fears are that I always want to provide a certain kind of life for my lady. I'm always going to be like that. But I think it's time for me to let my unhealthy fears go."

We headed home and talked on the phone almost until the sun came up. That night, our sights on each other transformed from friendship to letting out all the romantic feelings we'd felt for each other.

He'd already seen me without makeup, wearing sweatpants. He'd already heard his fair share of my bad dating stories. I'd already heard about some of the hard lessons he learned from a failed marriage. There wasn't any pretending left to do, so we spent time together; we met each other's families. We knew within a few weeks of dating we were going to marry each other.

We did sexy things like looking at each other's naked credit reports. There is nothing like showing your soon-to-be-spouse your credit report, nothing more revealing about the caliber of choices you've made in your life than when they have to see your credit card debt, your student loans, and your credit score.

On my birthday, after dating for nine months, Matt asked me to marry him. He proposed at the spot where we held hands on our first date. Well, not exactly at that spot. On our first date, we held hands at a beautiful fountain. Unfortunately for Matt's proposal plans, a couple arrived there before us, and they kissed each other's faces for so long that Matt finally gave up and proposed to me under the archway of an adjacent building. Thanks a lot, make-out couple! I hope the calories you burned during that make-out session were worth it!

CHAPTER 10

When Waiting Gets Weird

I lost my virginity in a hotel room. It was not like the movies, no dramatic musical crescendos, no perfectly crafted lines of dialogue, just two people cautiously traveling each other's bodies for the first time. I was thirty-one years old, and it was beautiful.

Like many church girls, I had signed a True Love Waits card when I was fourteen and started wearing a purity ring in high school. My church community supported me, and my group of friends, mostly virgins, gave me no peer pressure.

In college, I busied myself in campus ministry and avoided dating to keep my worst fear of getting pregnant before I got married from coming true. After college, I spent my spare time working with the college ministry at church. It was normal on our team of twenty or so twentysomethings for none of us to be getting any, so my abstinence was accepted, applauded, and encouraged. My virginity wasn't considered a freak of nature until I left my church bubble.

This is when I realized to be a virgin in my twenties, and quickly approaching my thirties, seemed strange, weird, and unfortunate to many people. I started working as an arts journalist, which changed my environment from church services to clubs and music venues. When strangers asked about my ring and I explained it was a symbol of my commitment to Jesus to wait until I got married to have sex, I was met with blank stares.

In my late twenties, my virginity turned into a worry. I wondered what grown man would want to marry a woman who had no sexual experience. A few potential dates applauded my choice. A couple of them tried a relationship with me, only to decide breaking up was the best thing to do. Some of them expressly let me know they did not date virgins and didn't want the responsibility, the clinging, or the baggage.

By the time I turned thirty, I was beginning to wonder if the status I had worn proudly as a ring on my finger had become a liability to be managed and cautiously explained. So I decided whether my number of partners was zero or infinity was no one's business, especially on a first date. If we made it past a few dates into something that had the potential for a relationship, then I could share my decision that I didn't want to have sex until marriage.

I wasn't ashamed of my choice, but I realized I didn't have to wear my virginity on my sleeve. My virginity wasn't the center of my worth. I realized that although fourteen-year-old me had signed a True Love Waits card, and high-school me put on a purity ring, I was an adult now. My decision to wait to have sex until I got married didn't have to be a platform for me to stand on. It was a personal, private journey between God and me. It was a decision I would wrestle with, feel good about, get frustrated with, pray about, cry about, and then feel peace about when I concluded that holding on to my virginity was something I really wanted to do: for God, for my future spouse and children, but also for myself.

I had seen and experienced enough abandonment, in my own family and among my friends. I wanted my first time having sex to be with a man who married me, wanted a family with me, and, like me, was living an imperfect life while growing and knowing Jesus.

When I told Matt, my then boyfriend, now husband, that I was a virgin, as we held hands on our first date, I waited to be rejected or made fun of. He didn't do either. He let me know that he respected and admired my choice and that, before we became friends, he had committed to remaining celibate until marriage.

A little more than a year from that first date, we stood across from each other in front of our friends and family and vowed to love, respect, and walk through all seasons of life together. I shared a beautiful first time with him on our honeymoon.

I don't regret waiting. I didn't all of a sudden feel like the heroine of some chick flick, but I felt sexy and beautiful and safe and loved. Not just because of the intimate experience I had with my husband, but also because I was learning to love myself and to support my own decisions.

There are a lot of things connected to sex: our souls, spirits, bodies, and emotions. There is a lot of guilt and shame shoveled at us for what we've done and sometimes for what we haven't done, for what was done to us, or what we've done to others. God never meant for sex or sexual experiences to be a dumping ground for guilt and shame.

The most important thing is letting what we do with our bodies and souls first become a personal conversation with the God who invented sex, created intimacy, and feels no shame about communicating with us about either. From there, we can make decisions that honor the God who made us in the first place and loves us unconditionally.

Part Three

Marriage

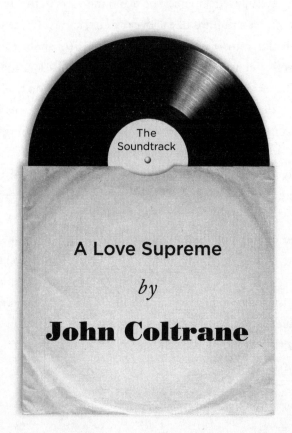

The Soundtrack

A Love Supreme

by

John Coltrane

I fell in love with John Coltrane after my college roommate handed me Coltrane's greatest hits CD to "borrow," and by "borrow," I'm certain she meant keep forever. For more than a decade, I have written all my poems to his music. This album only has four songs and is just over thirty minutes, but it will be some of the most amazing thirty minutes of your ears' life.

On "Acknowledgement," the piano thunders in the distance; the upright bass thumps like a lover's heart; and Coltrane's saxophone walks into the room to tell you a little about romance while softly chanting "a love supreme." On "Resolution," the bass whispers its story as Coltrane's sax and the piano take turns talking. "Pursuance" opens with a drum solo that seems like it will never end, tom and snare and high hat rumbling in rhythm. "Psalm" is haunting and moody, sad and intimate.

Playing the saxophone is the first musical thing I ever saw Matt do. There is nothing like seeing a musician pour his soul into the notes of an instrument. Coltrane expressed so much emotion while using little to no words at all. I have found a love supreme, and it means acknowledging love when it greets me, resolving to be vulnerable, continuing to pursue each other, and hoping the love we share writes a psalm befitting Song of Songs. It is a duet that is also a solo. It is bright notes and soft tones. It is finding the rhythm while learning to improvise.

CHAPTER 11

On Being a Terrible Bride

By the time I turned thirty, I think I had really come to believe I was never going to get married. I had stopped dreaming of a spouse or a wedding day or how many bridesmaids I'd have. This is why at thirty-one, about two weeks after getting used to the engagement ring Matt put on my finger, I woke up gasping at the fact that I must now plan a wedding.

Some of my friends walked into their engagements super prepared. They had hope chests and fabric swatches and cut-outs of their dream wedding dress from bridal magazines. I had nothing. No notebook, no magazines, no fantasy wedding ideas.

Matt was a youth pastor when we got engaged, so our church rallied around us, and thank God they did. If it hadn't been for them, we certainly would have eloped, and trust me when I say my grandma would not have let me hear the end of that. She would have smiled real nice and folded her hands into her lap when we told her we eloped. She would have said she was happy for us, but every so often for the next thirty years, when a commercial about a bridal shop came on or when a movie wedding scene played, she would have turned her head slightly to the side so I could see the tightness of her jawline and say, "Umph, it woulda been so nice to see you in your wedding dress walking down the aisle."

After saying this, she would straighten out the tablecloth and say, "I'm just glad y'all are happy." Which in Southern grandmother-speak means, "Girl, you stole my moment at your wedding away from me, and I'm not gonna let you forget it while I smile at you and say 'Bless your heart!'"

The women at the church rallied around me, ready to help. As quick and seemingly painless as eloping would have been, I was the first girl of my siblings and the first of my grandmother's granddaughters to get married. I wanted my family with us, and I wanted the youth group that Matt had been serving for years to attend our wedding. So we decided to have our wedding at the church. And the women at the church started asking me all the questions.

"What kind of flowers will you have? Roses? Calla lilies? Daisies? Birds of paradise? Do you want to have a candelabra? Will it be brass or iron? Gold or silver?"

Full and complete stop.

I'm not a flowers girl. Matt was the first man to ever give me a bouquet of flowers. This probably says more about the scalawags I was dating than it does my feelings about flowers, but let's not digress. I don't spend a lot of time outside. Did you know bugs are outside? Did you know there is a particular insect whose sole job it is to be drawn to flowers? I don't want to be near anything that a bug likes.

I don't hate flowers; I'm mostly just disinterested in them.

In fact, as I write this, I have only recently discovered my favorite flower. And I am well into my thirties. We were having a pot-luck outside with some people from our church, and the flowers surrounding the gazebo smelled like summer and spring and delicious, if it's possible for a flower to smell that way. The woman whose house was nearby said, "Those are gardenias." And now gardenias have changed my life. I mean, that smell is a perfect reason to go outside and risk being next to a bug. I actually considered planting gardenias at my own house until I realized I'd have to get soil on my hands, and then I rethought things.

If Matt and I were engaged now, I'd have a swift answer for the ladies at church. Gardenias! I want gardenias! They are amazing! But in that moment I didn't really care about flowers or candelabras. I just wanted to marry Matthew Owen because I thought he was fine and because God brought us together and because I thought we were going to have a good life.

I was far from bridezilla. I was the other end of that pendulum swing, the bride who has no idea what she wants because she is still adjusting to the fact that she is actually getting married instead of becoming a really cool nun. I had a minimal number of bridesmaids: my sister and my two best friends, who had been like sisters to me. I picked a color I liked, turquoise, and asked them to find dresses somewhat close to that.

"Doesn't matter to me where you get it or how much you spend; I just want you to choose something you like because you'll be stuck with this dress after my wedding, and I don't want you to blame me for picking a dress you hate," I said.

But to be honest, they probably still blame me, because where else can you wear a bright turquoise dress besides to another wedding?

I felt like a terrible bride, and I felt like less of a woman for not having more bride dreams than I did, for not being flower obsessed, for not being crafty enough to care about making my own centerpieces or designing my own dress or having all these cool ideas to turn my wedding into the YouTube event of the year.

Because I perform and speak at events for a living, I didn't want my wedding to be another event. Planning a big event didn't excite me. What made me happy was the idea that I was marrying a man I loved and trusted and could talk to about anything. I didn't have any doubt we were doing the right thing. God had a plan that included the two of us joining our lives together. *That* did excite me.

So I focused more on the life we were about to lead than on the one day that would be the beginning of our journey together. We hired a fantastic florist to make our centerpieces and bouquets, because while the women in my family write, speak, create, nurture, and care, we do not craft, and I didn't want to spend the night before my wedding making things none of us wanted to make. I wanted to spend it laughing and eating food with them, so we did.

A church let us borrow their iron candelabras. The women at our church took our miniscule food budget and, between Costco and their own kitchens, turned our wedding reception into a dessert haven of turquoise, with matching candles and fabric.

This is what people do when they love you and when they believe in the love you are walking into. Our simple and beautiful wedding, even with all the planning and stress, was way worth my grandma smiling at me rather than throwing me shade for the next thirty years.

There's no shame in enjoying wedding planning. There's no shame if you hated it like I did. The most important part is making sure you don't focus so much on the big day that you lose focus on the life you and your future spouse are about to build. The wedding is a great day. Your family is there. Your friends are there. A bunch of people who you will look at in the pictures later and not remember their names are there. But when the wedding day is over and people who say they love you have written embarrassing phrases and decorated your getaway car with things you don't want to discuss with your parents, when you drive off to your honeymoon, it's just you and your new spouse.

The two of you will have to figure out a whole lot more than what kind of flowers to have at your wedding or if the cake should be shaped like a heart or if cerulean is a good wedding color. You will have to navigate disagreements and the weird ways you were both raised and the tiny things that trigger your insecurities. You will fight over the smallest things. You will pray and sit in limbo over the biggest things. You will experience loss, grief, broke-ness, brokenness, wins, and losses.

You will learn things about each other you love. You will learn things about each other you absolutely do not like. You will give in. You will compromise. You will put your foot down. You will raise your voice. You will apologize. You will have many days when you feel like a bad spouse. You will learn every day, not what it means to be a generically good spouse, but what it means to be the spouse your spouse and marriage call for in that season.

Maybe one day I'll go outside and decide to plant those gardenias, and by "plant," I mean stand in the window and watch my husband do this.

CHAPTER 12

Letter to Myself on My Wedding Night

Dear Amena,

You are a wife now. This is not the same as graduating or getting a promotion or starting a business. This is not a checklist achievement. You are still yourself. Still the same girl who sings loud and hard when she is alone in her car. The girl who doesn't like to make the bed or wash the dishes.

Let's be honest. You're either rushing to read this because you can't wait to take off your clothes. Or you were in such a rush to take off your clothes that you forgot about this little letter and commenced to getting busy—and somewhere between knowing your husband in the way Abraham knew Sarah and getting an omelet for breakfast on your first morning as a married lady, you remembered to read this.

First of all, welcome to sex. You can totally see why everyone was doing it, right? Enjoy it. Take your time. Remember, you and your husband have your whole lives together. There's no need to rush. Unless you both want to because it's fun. If that's the case, then rush on, my sista! Otherwise, take your time. Sex is a language, and you're just learning your first words. Over time, you'll build enough of that language that you will have a lifetime of those words to say to each other.

Be present in the bedroom or the kitchen or the car or wherever the two of you find yourselves. Don't compare what's happening on your honeymoon or in your bedroom to anything you see on TV. On the one hand, real-life sex in your marriage will not be as cinematic or as blooper-free as screenwriters imagine. You will have many hilarious "oops" stories to tell that will mostly remain between you and your husband and the occasional trusted friend who wouldn't be highly freaked out by this information.

On the other hand, TV and the movies can't truly capture how devastatingly beautiful many of your bedroom moments will be. Even the best screenwriters can't truly express what it's like for two people who love each other and share both the intimacy that has nothing to do with sex and all of the intimacy that makes sex the life-changing force it is. Poets, musicians, painters, and sculptors have all failed to fully illustrate and describe the all-encompassing journey it is to traverse each other's bodies and experience pleasure in all the ways God created.

So don't expect your new sex life to be anything like what you've seen on screen. But don't be surprised when your new sex life is better than fiction. As a side note, don't forget to buy lingerie every now and then. Not just because your husband likes it either. Remember to buy yourself lingerie, the kind *you* like. Married sex isn't just about pleasing your spouse; it's also about knowing what you like and enjoy and about having a mutually enjoyable experience.

People will tell you marriage is work. When you hear the word *work*, you will equate it to the knot you kept in your stomach working that corporate job you hated. It will remind you of shuffling papers, completing assignments and projects you cared nothing about, working with people you only stomached because you had to.

Marriage is music. Less cubicle and more dance floor. Some seasons you will dance so close you can feel each breath tap the nape of your neck. You will hold each other, shoulder and waist, as if the earth's axis depended on the rhythm your hips can keep. The two of you will become the muse for the greatest love song you will ever create.

Some seasons you will find yourselves wounded, by life and by each other. The dirge of grief and hardship will press so heavily on your backs you will find yourselves at opposite sides of the room, pressed into a doorjamb, as if your shoulders can prevent suffering from pushing its way into your rhythm. You will learn how dirge can become second line, how grief holds hands with joy. You will learn to find and clutch each other's fingertips, no matter the rhythm of the song.

Whatever your season, find your rhythm every day. Don't wait until you feel like it. Don't wait until life and the world have choked out the very sound of the two of you. Tune your ear to the music of your marriage every day. Make space to listen to your spouse, even if it means you must turn down the noise of your life. Leave each other the space to grow and become. Don't assume you know everything about your spouse. Discover new things about each other. You will remain the same people, yet in so many ways, you will grow into new people, and you will have to relearn how to love.

Your friend Elizabeth was right. In marriage, there are two ways to hang curtains and wash dishes and make the bed and cook dinner and drive the car and work and create. There are two ways to put the toilet paper on the roll, but for the sake of peace in your house, pretend there is only one if your spouse feels strongly about it.

You will hurt each other's feelings. You will make each other mad. You will get on each other's last nerve. You will say things you *don't* mean. You will say mean things you *do* mean. You will be triggered to defend yourself or walk out on an argument or shut down or yell or cry. Your husband will say one thing and you will hear something completely different, because there's still an eight-year-old girl inside of you trying to heal old wounds. You will have to explain this to your spouse, and this will be one of the most vulnerable things you can do.

You will wonder if your marriage is as far along as it should be. You will use a terrible meter to measure this: social media or the small part of the picture people share with you without sharing all the challenges and difficulties they met along the way. You will wonder if your marriage is normal and if you fight more than you should, as much as you should, the way you should.

Remember there is no normal. A healthy marriage is a life of two imperfect, wounded people walking with God as he heals their woundedness and shows them his love through their love—and sometimes through their lack of love. God is with you. He will teach you everything you need to know.

No one truly knows what happens behind the closed doors of a marriage except the two people in it and God. Don't judge. Don't compare. Don't covet. Don't be jealous. Be present. Be honest. Be your full self: broken, bruised, loved, and accepted.

Don't forget to laugh. To make out. To wear that lipstick or those high heels that make you feel your most Beyoncé-est. Pray for each other. Ask God, the inventor of love, to show you how to love your spouse and how to be loved by your spouse.

I know you have to go now. You're on your honeymoon, which is the sex equivalent of football training. You are probably at least going for two-a-days. You need to rest up for that. Trust me.

Enjoy each other. Hold each other. Be right where you are and nowhere else. Build a life together—one day, one moment, one handhold at a time.

Love,
Your future self

CHAPTER 13

The Worst Marriage Advice

There are two times in your life when you are most susceptible to being told scary stories disguised as advice: before you get married and before you have your first child. Seasoned married couples and experienced mothers must think it's their duty to warn you about the horror that could be ahead of you. This must be their version of keeping it real, which is unfortunate for us first-timers.

Yes, we are in love. Yes, we hope our marriage will be like Meredith and Derek's from *Grey's Anatomy* before things got weird in season 11. Yes, we are probably really idealistic about everything because we're just beginning, but not all of our ideals are wrong. We might be more in need of a hug and a word of encouragement than the sharp needle in a balloon deflating our dreams and desires for our future.

Tell us we can make it. Tell us it will be hard but God is with us and we can do it. Tell us you still like your spouse. Tell us you still kiss. Tell us even with all the hell on earth you've been through that you'd do it all over again. Tell us something hopeful that will help us keep our heads up when the tough days come. Whatever you do, please don't give the following pieces of terrible marriage advice.

"Never let your left hand know what your right hand is doing."

This is actually a quote from Jesus in Matthew 6, but as a child, I overheard my grandma and her friends sharing this marriage advice like a plate of biscuits and molasses. Jesus was referring to how we should give to the needy, but when my grandma and her friends said this phrase, it was always in reference to a man. A no-good, dirty-dog, trifling man. The kind of man who merited a woman keeping extra cash under her mattress, in her box of maxi pads, in a secret bank account that said trifling man didn't know anything about.

When they used this phrase, the woman in question was the right hand and the no-good man was the left hand. Sometimes the man couldn't be trusted because he didn't see a woman's body as sacred enough not to violate with violence. Sometimes he couldn't be trusted because he gambled, smoked, or drank away every dollar within a tiny radius of his fingertips, leaving the woman no choice but to hide money to take care of herself and possibly her children.

An older church mother gave me this advice before I married Matt. She was fond of Matt, so she wanted the opportunity to sniff me out and test my motivations. The main way she did this was by asking me out to lunch, which meant me picking her up to run her errands and eating lunch at a restaurant of her choice.

She told me her own love stories. She had loved twice in her life: once with the love of her life, who passed away before their love could see the future they'd both dreamed of, and once with a man whose words said he loved her but whose actions were those of a thief and con artist.

On one of our last lunch meetings before she approved enough of me to give me her wedding veil and a set of cast-iron skillets (I still cook with them today), she pressed twenty dollars into my hand.

"Don't you tell Matt about this. You don't let your left hand know what your right hand is doing!" she said.

I was never good at keeping secrets, so Matt and I used the money to go to the movies.

"If you're a woman who wants to get and stay married, domesticate yourself."

When Matt and I were engaged, a man asked me, "So, now that you're getting married, you're gonna stop traveling, right?"

"No, I'll still be traveling. It's my job," I said.

"Oh, I was just thinking since you're about to get married, maybe you'd slow down your travel schedule a bit."

These are comments women field all the time, comments a man our same age with our same job and same station in life would never have to field. He'd never have to answer for why he wasn't reducing his surgery schedule or slowing down his corporate climb for his marriage.

I wish I could tell you I spewed the proper amount of women's empowerment back to this man, but I didn't. I answered as plainly as I could, and I went to my car and cried. I was trying to juggle a lot. I was not only trying to find my way as a creative, an entrepreneur, and an artist, but I was also trying to find my way as the future wife of a pastor on staff at our local church.

I am a rule follower. I'm much better at meeting other people's expectations than finding my own voice and bravery. I wanted to be the perfect youth pastor's wife, whatever that meant.

This man's sideways comment made me question myself, made me wonder if I could continue to be a full-time artist and have a good marriage. Maybe both weren't possible. Maybe I needed to buy an apron and find a really good blueberry muffin recipe.

I said all of this to Matt through tears on the phone. I wanted to know what he expected of me, what I was getting into.

"You're not marrying that guy. You're marrying me. I'm marrying you because I want to spend my life with you, all of you. That includes what God is calling you to do in your career. I'm not here to squelch anything God gave you. I want you to fly," he said.

Hearing Matt say those words confirmed what I knew was true. I was making a great choice in a husband, and that moment taught me it's not up to anyone else to define for my husband and me how our household or our relationship works. The beauty of marriage is that it is a unique experience based on the two people who stood at the altar and vowed to live no longer as two but as one.

Since then, Matt and I have had to prayerfully consider a lot of choices, opportunities, hurdles, and obstacles. We have had to re-center ourselves on what God says, on what God asks of us, not on what society or other people's expectations say we should be or do.

When I think back on this man's comments, sometimes I

wonder if the best response would have been to not even dignify his sexist comment with a reply. Or if my best response should have involved the most eloquent mix of curse words I could think of.

"Don't handle marital disputes like a rookie."

At a wedding reception Matt deejayed, this sweet couple (bless their hearts) decided to offer an open-floor time during the toasts. This always goes badly. Remember how on *Sesame Street* one of the kids was doing his own thing and one of the kids was not the same? There's always someone like this at a wedding, stewing about their own struggling love life, waiting to be offered a mic to rain on the parade or spray Raid on the cake, as it were.

This bride and groom had already heard from their parents, friends, and family members, all with well-wishes and funny but not terribly embarrassing stories to tell. There was a lull in the flow of people volunteering to speak. This probably would have been a great time to cut the cake, but before the moment could be cut short, a woman marched up to grab the mic with her piece of advice for the newlyweds. She cut through the crowd as if she was Sophia in the movie *The Color Purple* about to ask Miss Celie, "You told Harpo to beat me?"

"People say don't go to bed angry, but I don't listen to that because I ain't no rookie," she said.

Please know that she landed on the word *rookie* with the blunt force of a sweaty Southern preacher yelling right before the organist starts playing the shout music. I honestly don't remember anything else she said because I was stuck on the word *rookie* for the next five minutes.

Matt and I had our first married fight in the Art Institute of Chicago because this must be what two artists do: have their first fight while looking at amazing art. I had been touring with Gungor, and Matt and I had been apart for two and a half weeks. I flew to Chicago to speak at Wheaton College, and Matt flew from Atlanta to spend the weekend with me before I had to head back to the tour bus.

It was such a great day. We held hands and walked Chicago's busy streets. We shopped. We ate Chicago pizza the first day and decided on the second day to eat a Chicago hot dog. It was St. Patrick's Day, so the river was green. Since it was the middle of the day, most people were only slightly inebriated. Somewhere after the hot dog and before dusk, we walked through the Art Institute, holding hands, whispering sweet nothings, and having intellectual, artsy conversation.

And then Matt said something. It was meant to be off the cuff, a hypothetical thought, a point for dialogue or conversation. It quickly disintegrated into me being offended, him being caught off guard, and both of us putting up the quickest walls we could muster to separate us from each other.

Getting into an argument when you haven't seen each other in weeks and you have only two days together before you'll be apart again is the worst. There's a part of you that wants to forget the argument because you really don't have time for it. You want to spend the time you have together celebrating, having sex, and being romantic. You don't want to spend the time hashing out what you meant, what he sounded like he meant, why that triggered you, what you learned from your parents about how to handle conflict. So we spent the next two hours walking around Chicago, traveling the tightrope of silence and faux politeness.

Somewhere around the Magnificent Mile, my stomach began a conversation with me, a conversation that reminded me of Sigourney Weaver in *Alien*, when the alien baby was trying its best to jump out of her skin. Something was very wrong. Something in my stomach wanted out, and I had a feeling it was that hot dog. I had a feeling if we'd had any friends in Chicago, they probably would have told us not to go to *that* hot dog place, but we were two people in love trying to be tourists, trying not to waste the small amount of time we had with each other by fighting.

Our awkward silence and visible annoyance with each other faded quickly when we realized neither one of us was feeling well. We bought sodas, hoping the carbonation would help calm our digestive systems, but whatever had gone wrong in my stomach wanted out, and there would be no holding it in.

The streets and sidewalks were crowded with mostly drunk people now, so when I leaned over the edge of the sidewalk and for the first time in my life threw up in public, the St. Patrick's Day patrons cheered me on in what they thought was drunken exuberance. This made Matt so angry, he yelled back, "She doesn't feel good!"

We spent that night alternating between bathroom visits and rehashing our argument. We had food poisoning that lingered for a few days after the hot dog incident. We were certainly rookies. Pro tip: don't fight and have food poisoning at the same time. If you have the opportunity, just choose one. It's really difficult to focus on them both.

We headed to the airport the next day—Matt to fly back to Atlanta and me to Denver to meet up with the Gungor band for the second leg of the tour. Matt felt terrible sending me on a plane alone feeling so badly. He made sure I had all the sports drinks, Pepto Bismol, and crackers I could carry.

A few days later, when I could finally hold down food, we brought our first married fight to resolve. I learned I needed to listen to what he actually was saying, not what I assumed he was saying by adding words and intent based on my own hurtful experiences. He learned to see things from my perspective and began to understand how what he intended to be a harmless statement could trigger hurt and angry feelings in me. We both apologized. We both had to learn to not make each other the enemy, even when our insecurities said we should do so.

It's okay to be a marriage rookie. Marriage is about being willing to constantly learn you may be wrong; you may need to change; you may need to grow up; you may need healing in some areas. It's about not running away from what you have to face in yourself.

Years from now, when some rookie couple decides to open the floor to their whole wedding reception to share words on their new nuptials, I'm gonna take the mic from the best man and tell this story. I'll take way longer than the story deserves, and I'll tell them, *I don't fight with my man while I have food poisoning because I ain't no rookie.* And then I'll cut myself a huge slice of their wedding cake because I'm not a wedding guest rookie either.

CHAPTER 14

Marriage Boot Camp

A few weeks into my engagement to Matt, right as I was getting used to the weight of the ring on my finger and beginning to feel the stress of planning a wedding, Kimberly had another proposal for me.

"My husband and I just got back from this marriage boot camp, and we signed you and Matt up to go."

She smiled at me because she knew her sentence had just gotten on my nerves. She knows me well enough to know I am almost always not going to be interested in anything that has the phrase "boot camp" in it unless donuts and cupcakes are involved.

Nevertheless, a couple weeks later, Matt and I found ourselves in a room with two boot camp facilitators and two other couples. No cupcakes. No donuts. One couple, who I'll call Sam and Diane, had been dating for years, but the boyfriend was in the military, so they'd spent a lot of their relationship apart. No matter what exercise we did, Sam's face always looked like he was in a dentist's office waiting room, and Diane looked like she was about to start whining but thought better of it. The boot camp was their decision maker to see if they should get married.

The other couple was a pastor and his wife, who I'll call James and Florida. James walked like a linebacker and spoke with the staccato of someone who was used to telling other people what to do. Florida talked like a preacher only until James started to talk. Before James could say five words, Florida started spraying words as if her tongue was a verbal assault rifle. They had been married ten years and were on the brink of divorce. The boot camp was a last-ditch effort to save their marriage.

Matt and I missed the first day because of work. The second day, we walked into a room that had the tension of an emotional war zone. Sam and Diane sat in a corner whispering to each other, and James and Florida were on opposite sides of the room, as if they were opposing boxers preparing for the next round. For the next two hours, they yelled at each other and stormed in and out of the room during each exercise.

So far we'd learned, even though they were at each other's throats, James enjoyed Florida's spaghetti but wished she'd clean the house more; they'd managed to have sex the night before; and Florida was tired of dealing with James. By the time lunch arrived, we were tired of dealing with both of them. The other couple had disappeared, so it was just the four of us.

"While you're at lunch, your homework assignment is to brag on your spouse," the facilitator said. "The four of you are going to lunch together."

I have never dreaded a Chick-fil-A meal more than I dreaded that one. James and Florida offered to drive—as if we really wanted to spend more time with them.

After we all had our sweet teas, lemonades, and lunches, Matt and I decided to launch into the homework because we didn't want to leave these two any chances to make this lunch more awkward for us. Surprisingly, James went first, bragging about how smart Florida was. As each of us took turns sharing how awesome our partners are, we could feel the tension at the table releasing to a sense of calm.

The next day, we learned how to tango. The other couple had mysteriously returned. (I still feel they owe me a stress-free Chick-fil-A lunch.) Before our tango lesson, we had to switch partners and learn how to dance with one of the other people there. We stepped on each other's toes. We laughed. We were patient and spoke gently to each other. Then we switched back to our own partners, and the tensions between the partners of the other two couples returned. It's interesting how dancing brings out all the places we don't trust our partner with our rhythm, our feet, or our heart.

After our tango lesson, the facilitator sat us down to debrief us. We were all kinder and gentler when we weren't dancing with our own partner. It was easier to be kind to a stranger than it was to be kind to someone who had disappointed or hurt us.

The moment I remember most from our marriage boot camp experience was a comment Florida made to me while we sat on the steps during our last break. She looked at me looking at Matt from afar while he talked with James. "Keep talking to each other," she said. "What's happening between me and James is what happens when ten years go by and you don't talk through anything." I don't know what happened to James and Florida, if they were able to find a way to make their relationship work, or how they were able to juggle the strain of their ministry and their marriage.

All these years later though, I think of James and Florida when I don't want to do the work of communicating to Matt what's really going on with me, when I'd rather watch TV instead of listen. In those moments when I put my phone down so I can listen to my husband share his heart with me, I realize that James and Florida gave us a gift. They were our personal teachers of what not to do. The pain in their eyes left such a strong impression on me I decided I'd rather sit down and be vulnerable with Matt than someday have to look across the room and realize my partner had become my opponent.

CHAPTER 15

Marriage Lessons

It wasn't long into my relationship with Matt before I learned a few important things I would need to know as his wife. It also didn't take long for me to realize most of Matt's marriage requirements center around making sure I understand his definition of proper food portions.

Don't split the soup.

On one of our first dates, we sat near another couple. When the server came to their table, the woman placed her order and said, "We'll split the soup." Matt turned to me and said, "No. Never split the soup. No one wants to be with someone who wants to split the soup."

Never go to Waffle House without alerting your spouse.

The first year we were married, we lived in a small, crappy, two-bedroom apartment. Our second bedroom was filled with instruments, turntables, and sound equipment, so most days I wrote from the kitchen table, as I had done before we were married. But the trouble with writing at the kitchen table when I lived with my favorite person on the planet was I spent more time talking than writing, so I began to camp out at my local coffee place. I wrote out my insecurities and frustrations, hit my word count for the day, and returned home. When I walked in the door one day, Matt gave me a hug and sniffed me.

"Where you been?" he asked.

"At the coffee spot, writing, like I told you," I said with an attitude brewing.

He sniffed me again.

"You don't smell like you've been at a coffee shop."

My mind raced, wondering who I'd been duped into marrying. How had I missed this controlling side of him? Where was my passport? Was I in the middle of a Lifetime movie?

"You smell like you've been to Waffle House," he said.

"No, I did not go to Waffle House. I smell like coffee, like burnt coffee after sitting in a coffee place for hours."

"Oh, okay. All I'm saying is if you are going to Waffle House, just let me know first in case I want to go. Or at least call me and see if I want you to order something for me."

Don't split the dessert.

Sometimes when we go out to eat, I want to split the dessert, mainly because my digestive desires are almost always larger than my actual capacity to eat food. So I ask my husband to split the dessert with me. He smiles and says words like, "Sure," "Yep," "Anything for you, girl," but what he means is, "If I didn't love you and lie in a bed next to you, I would never agree to this, because I want every piece of cake, every spoonful of pudding, every chocolate chip in the chocolate chip cookies TO MYSELF."

We have recently agreed the best dessert plan is for each person to order his or her own dessert, and if I decide not to finish mine, he may be willing to help me out. For fraction purposes, my husband would rather have one and a half desserts than a half dessert.

There is a sixth love language.

Matt cares about spending quality time together, and he likes a good gift or an act of service. But the true way to his heart is a fantastically fried piece of chicken. I hope Gary Chapman reads this before he writes his next edition of *The Five Love Languages*. This will probably help a lot of relationships.

CHAPTER 16

The Mystery
of Marriage

After splitting their honeymoon between Universal Studios and the king-sized bed in their resort room, they returned home to their crappy apartment. The only apartment where, as two stressed-out people with limited income and less-than-stellar credit, they were accepted and could afford to live. The apartment whereupon move-in they discovered extra roommates of the six-legged kind. The bold kind of roommates that sometimes wait until it's dark to have parties on the kitchen counter and then scatter when they see fluorescent lights.

As he unlocked the door to the apartment, the odor of bug spray was thick in the air. All of their wedding gifts had been moved into a clumsy circle in the middle of the room so the pest control technician could spray the perimeter.

They had returned home, but their honeymoon hadn't ended. They opened each gift and card and oohed and aahed at their new life that now included a blender, a waffle maker, and casserole dishes.

One card etched itself into her memory. Her husband's sister, now her sister-in-law, had written in her card to them she hoped they would discover the mystery of marriage. Only being eleven days married, she had no idea what any of this would mean.

There is much mystery to how they survived those extra roommates and a beat-up secondhand couch. How they learned to carry the weight of local church ministry and the rigor of touring, traveling, and performing as artists. How "pillow talk" is such an inadequate term for the safe place their nighttime conversations became to each other, a place where they could admit when they had been wrong or wronged, when they were full of insecurity or pride, when they wanted to laugh until their eyes watered but no one else would have laughed except this person they were lying in bed next to.

His youth pastor job ended, so they went into business together. They moved out of their crappy apartment into a place that had large windows where they could watch the trees change their dance with each season. They discovered the pain of medical diagnoses and countless doctor's appointments. They found out although faith seems like it should be the surest thing to put your trust in, it often feels like so much water beneath the feet of Peter, desperate to be sure it is really Jesus calling you out of your boat and onto the water. They learned to take care of each other, to take better care of themselves.

They bought a home together. Two people who had lived transient lives finally put down roots. They experienced the joy of pregnancy, only to have the blissfulness stolen from them before they could see the eyes of the little one they had yet to meet. They still carry that grief. There are still certain times of the year when they both slow down and let the tears come as often and as much as they'd like.

There is much mystery to how two people can survive this and still find themselves holding hands and each other after so much hope was lost. Still find themselves holding on to a hope between them that neither one of them can completely say out loud.

She does not know what it's like to have a man to stick by her side at all times through all things. He has only known marriage that meant you say words like *together* but you will really be alone. They show up for each other. They inevitably fail each other too. He teaches her about grace, and she teaches him what it means for someone to believe in him.

They do not know where life will take them next. They do not know if their future will include little ones or if they will look around and realize it will always be the two of them after all. They are hanging curtains and putting up picture frames. He comes downstairs and plays the piano, and she tells him everything she dreams about—the sleeping dreams and the awake ones too.

So much time has passed, and yet they have so much time to look forward to. She prays for the music on the inside of him to make its way out of his chest and into his fingers. He prays for her body and her soul to find the rest and healing God meant for her. He doesn't want her shoulders to know burdens. She doesn't want his chest to know what it feels like to be beaten down by the negative words in the world.

She feels like love should be a bigger word to describe how his very being has healed her and softened her and helped her grow into the woman God created her to be. This word has the weight of the cross and the flight of the resurrection written into its letters. Maybe English is not its first language.

He has so many ways he wants to show her this word, wants to prove to her he will protect her, take care of her, work hard for her. He wants to be her hero in so many perfectly imperfect ways.

Tonight they will rest worn bones and weary souls right next to each other. She will put her hand on his chest and fall asleep to the rhythm of his breathing.

Part Four

Lessons in Adulting

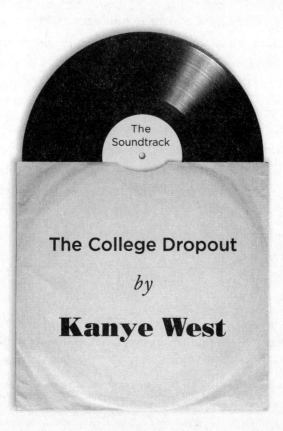

The Soundtrack

The College Dropout

by

Kanye West

My brother, Robert, and I talk about a lot of things: relationships, family, and God. But the thing we probably talk about the most is hip-hop, and one night he told me about a new rapper I needed to hear. "His name is Kanye, Mena. He got into this bad car accident and had to have his jaw wired shut, and then he recorded a song called 'Through the Wire'!"

This was several months before any of us knew how Kanye West would change the sound of hip-hop with his hungry, self-deprecating verses and soulful production on his debut album *The College Dropout*.

When I first heard Kanye, I was a recent college grad, working my first buttoned-up corporate job, trying to decide if I should surrender to working for the man or make a path for myself as an entrepreneur. Kanye rapped about hating his former retail job, about struggle, about beating the odds and statistics, about needing Jesus to walk with you while the devil is trying to bring you down. This album reminded me not to miss out on seeing my dreams become a reality, not to miss out on what can happen when you take a risk to do something refreshing and creative. Kanye's music was with me when I learned some of my first lessons in adulting.

Kanye has been through a lot since then. He lost his mom. He got married and became a father. He also has become a polarizing figure, someone whom people either love or vehemently hate. I hope he finds peace for his soul. I hope he rediscovers his voice. I hope he'll listen back to young Kanye's words sometime and be encouraged.

CHAPTER 17

The Power
of Yes

I love yes. Yes is so awesome. Yes makes everyone like you, and it makes everyone happy. Would you like fries with that? Yes. Will you marry me? Yes. Do you have room for dessert? Yes. Always yes. Can you do me a favor? Yes. Can I borrow twenty dollars? Yes.

TV creator and producer Shonda Rhimes wrote an entire book about yes (*Year of Yes*), and on the strength of *Grey's Anatomy*, *Scandal*, and *How to Get Away with Murder* alone, I would do a large percentage of everything she says. Shonda was right about a couple of things, and yes, we are on a first-name basis. Olivia Pope can fix just about anything except her own love life, and there is power in yes.

Yes is important, but not for the reasons I assumed it would be. For me, yes was a key to the land of people-please. It was the small bottle that read, "Drink me," that led me to do more than I should, more than I could. Yes led me to date men who couldn't commit to me. Yes said to be Christian meant to be busy "doing things for God." Yes led me to finding as many things to do on a Friday night as I could because I couldn't stand to be alone.

Yes is when my date arrived forty-five minutes late and still on his phone and I smiled while he took another ten minutes to finish his call. Yes is being scared to order what I actually want for lunch because I'm afraid I'll sound like Meg Ryan from *When Harry Met Sally*. Yes is not knowing when to say I've had enough freshly ground pepper, enough cheese, enough disregard, enough ridicule.

When I was a kid, I took yes too far. My mom shopped at Sam's once a month. Mom's bulk grocery purchases were an exciting place for a kid growing up in the 1980s. Twenty boxes of Tang, two tubs of Neapolitan ice cream, fifteen bags of Gushers, four jars of pickles, two family-size packs of Honeycombs, seven boxes of Capri Sun, twenty Fruit Roll-ups, eight six-packs of Pepsi, and five bags of chips, and I tasted them all. Yes, I had at least a spoonful or sip of *everything* until I made myself sick. I said yes to such a wide variety of snacks, drinks, and food that my stomach spent the night yelling its displeasure. It didn't matter to me if they went together, if they made a meal, if they were nutritious. What mattered most was that I tasted everything. I learned to say yes with desperation, as if it would all disappear in the morning.

Yes doesn't have to be said out of scarcity. It doesn't have to be the place I hide behind a polite smile when I really want to say no. Yes doesn't have to be a false sense of security where I fear saying no to people—whether they are family members or people whom I have just met—because their love and approval are attached to whether I say yes to their every request. That's not what love is.

Yes is not something to be given away to everyone. Yes can be treasured, valued, considered. Yes can be selective. Saying yes isn't about being a good person. Saying yes is about people, places, things, opportunities that deserve it and will appreciate it. Yes costs me something, and this is a cost I should weigh carefully.

By giving us free will, God offers us the power of yes. He wants us to give our thought-out yes to him. He doesn't want our fake yes, our "I better say yes." He wants our real yes. Because I want to. Because I love you. Yes.

Sometimes I also need to say yes to myself. Yes to drinking water. Yes to getting rest. Yes to exercising. Yes to eating biscuits sometimes, because why else would God give us the ability to make flour if it weren't to make and eat biscuits? Yes to spending time with people who refresh and encourage me. Yes to being still and quiet before God. Yes to dancing and bobbing my head to music that reminds me I am alive. Yes to inspiration. Yes to cackling.

I am learning I can say yes out of abundance, not out of depletion. If I don't say yes to God and yes to taking care of myself, then I don't have any healthy yeses to give to the people and things I care about.

Yes to cooking food with love in the crust and the sauce. Yes to folding clothes in the homes of my friends who are new mamas and talking to their babies about hip-hop while Mom takes a much-needed shower. Yes to listening to my grandma explain the importance of owning an ankle-length trench coat, even when I know I'm not going to buy one. Yes to walking alongside my people when they hurt, when they grieve, when they are struggling with pain or disease, and yes to letting them walk alongside me.

Saying yes reminds me to be honored when I receive a yes and to feel the good weight of it when I give one.

CHAPTER 18

The Power of No

Nice girls don't say no. They smile. They are polite and accommodating. Only a certain kind of woman says no, and those kinds of women have been characterized by a word that rhymes with *hitches*.

I was raised as a Southern girl to be demure, to throw shade sweetly, to speak in covert language like "bless his heart" when you really mean #$&%!!! I was not raised to say no.

No is mean and selfish. No is rude and uncouth. No is a thing you can only get away with if you wear a certain brand of boss lady pants and happen to be standing at the front of a boardroom, banging your fist on the table and saying phrases like, "We are not meeting our strategic objectives!" or "That is *not* in your wheelhouse!" or "Who invented panty hose anyway?!" and even then you can barely skate by with saying no.

No is actually none of those things. No is a barometer for how much a person respects you. A person's no deserves immediate respect. No is great at setting boundaries. No is not a coy game of "tag, you're it" or playing hard to get. No doesn't mean yes; it always and unequivocally means no. Any person who hears your no and assumes it is a door ajar and not a door closed and locked is wrong.

McGruff the Crime Dog was right. Just say no. To drugs. When you don't want to be touched. When you are being disrespected. When you are offered mediocre cookies. Life is entirely too short to suffer mediocre cookies.

I am learning to say no to shoes that don't fit; to clothes I still wear because they used to fit, even though they aren't my size anymore; to weighing myself when I am emotional, hormonal, or have eaten several carbs. No to spending time with people who offer me backhanded compliments, as if they are doing me a favor. No to more small talk than real talk. No to helping anyone more than they want to help themselves.

Sometimes we must say no even to good things. No to helping someone in need when we can barely take the time to eat or rest ourselves. No to the church busyness we have equated with holiness. No to meetings, committees, organizations, and extracurricular activities that leave our already too full schedules without downtime or margin. Doing good things isn't always best, especially if doing "good" things means you can't take proper care of yourself, care for your family, and grow closer to God.

I learned a great lesson about the connection between being a businesswoman and saying no from Beyoncé and Oprah. We were sitting down talking about our respective careers. Okay, well, I was sitting down watching them on television, and they were sitting down talking to each other, but basically we were having dinner at Oprah's house.

Beyoncé: Business and polite don't match.
Oprah: Amen to that, sister!
Amena reaches to high-five them through the TV screen.
Beyoncé: People just push you as far as you allow them.
I'm learning that you can be kind and be strong,
but I have to be fair to myself.

For nearly a decade, I have lived in the tension of being an artist and an entrepreneur. Being an artist and a business owner has taught me the power of saying no. I'm learning to take responsibility for my choices, to not compromise my values or my artistic integrity. I'm learning to say no, even if it means less money, less popularity, fewer likes. It is not anyone's job to tell me how awesome I am or feed the insatiable beast that is my human insecurity. It is not my job to bend and wield myself to the whims of an audience, a stage, or a paycheck.

My only job is to be myself, to be the woman, artist, entrepreneur God created me to be. If I am asked to be anything other than that or to do anything other than that, the answer is no. Sometimes that feels impolite. But I am learning, like Beyoncé and Oprah (and all of us), I can remain humble and kind and still say no. No to wedging myself into the small box of anyone's expectations. No to trying to be anyone other than myself. No to building my identity on anything other than being a daughter of God.

This is easy to type and much more challenging to do. I must constantly lay down the weight of opinion, the chokehold of pride, the race of comparison. It is saying no to my own selfishness, no to trying my best to be god instead of walking with and learning from God how to be who he created me to be.

Sometimes people we love or care about or want to like us have a hard time taking no for an answer. Maybe because they are used to hearing yes, and an all-of-a-sudden no shocks them. Maybe because no doesn't serve their purposes. Maybe because they were taught no was a curse word, and it offends them. Either way, it may be hard for them, and they may not respond well. But they deserve a no nonetheless. Loving someone doesn't mean we can't say no to them. If we love them and they love us, they should be able to hear no and respect it, with no explanations ad nauseam as to why we can't do what they think we should do.

God understands the power of no. He is not a constant Yes God. Sometimes when God says no, it will hurt. It will sting. I will beg God to explain. Sometimes he never gives an explanation. In other moments, time will be the greatest explainer of all. Sometimes we ask God for things and he says no because he knows we can't handle what we're asking for. Because he knows what we're asking for isn't his best for us. Because it isn't time. Because it isn't good. Because God always knows better than we do.

Practice saying no until it no longer feels mean and unfriendly. Practice taking no for an answer. You may not ever want to be best friends with no, but learn to partner with it. Learn to use its power for good. Let no help you build healthy boundaries. Let no teach you how to trust God more. Let no show you the power of saying yes and meaning it.

CHAPTER 19

Reasons Why Social Media Is the Best Thing That Ever Happened to Me

I got my first email address when I was fifteen: my rap name plus my birthday at aol.com. I used email on a regular basis for the first time when I entered college and got my first .edu address. I graduated from college before I joined Myspace, and I was working my first full-time job with benefits before I joined Facebook. Three years after Twitter started, I begrudgingly set up an account after a friend spent hours convincing me I *needed* to do it. A few years ago, I joined Instagram, because who doesn't want to filter their pictures and pretend for a small moment they are an awesome photographer?

Social media has come such a long way from the AOL days. No one has to endure the weird screech of the modem dialing up. No one has to wait for a CD-ROM to arrive in the mail before they can access the web. No one has to be chained to their desktop to check their email.

Here are a few amazing things social media has brought to my life:

I have an excuse to be nosy.

Nosy used to be relegated to Pearl from the apartment building and sitcom *227*. The show aired in the late 1980s, starring Marla Gibbs from *The Jeffersons*, comedian Jackée Harry, and newcomer Regina King, who is now an acting/directing phenom. Helen Martin played an elderly woman named Pearl, who spent most of the show touting her wisdom and wit from the window of her apartment. She was unashamedly nosy and paid no attention to the phrase "that ain't none of my business."

I am the Pearl of my social media. I scroll my newsfeed sometimes for the sole purpose of being nosy. When someone posts something controversial or offensive, I click on the comments section and grab some popcorn like I'm at the movies. When people break up, I look at each of their timelines to see if they have deleted their couple pictures yet. Thank you, social media, for helping me to be nosy from the convenience of my couch.

I can distantly keep in touch with people I can't or don't want to have coffee with.

So far on social media, I've been able to keep in touch with my old boss, my childhood friends from elementary and junior high school in two different cities, and coworkers I loved from a job I hated. Social media is a conglomeration of all the people you think about from time to time but never want to have in the same room at a dinner party.

I get to see pictures of their kids and grandkids, how they celebrate their anniversaries, when they get a new job, their quirky answers to ridiculous quizzes. I learn if they are religious, political, fun, or serious. I can decide how many of their posts I want to see or if I want to remain connected to them without seeing their posts at all.

If we were to sit down for coffee, I might discover many of these people who were nice to me when I was younger might not even like who I am now, and I might not be able to tolerate who they've become. But we don't have to sit down for coffee. We only have to see pictures of each other's gardens and sandwiches sometimes. I can totally handle that. I can wish them well without having to endure any awkwardness. Awesome.

I can be international now.

I have a passport with a couple of stamps in it, but I don't have a lifestyle of international travel. Although if you are reading this and you would like to help fund this lifestyle, I am accepting all donations. Social media allows me to follow people from places I have never been. I learn about fashion in Nigeria, the poetry community in Germany, nightlife in Dubai, shopping in England.

When world events happen, my social media timeline tells me about protests, tragedies, injustices, and how I can help, give, or spread the word. Even global news can be found more quickly and sometimes more truthfully from social media than through traditional media outlets. I can learn from the people I follow who live and work in other countries how to be a better global citizen.

I can learn from people who are different from me.

My social media timeline is a diverse assortment of people. I follow people of various religions and those who ascribe to no religion. My timeline includes artists, scientists, parents, journalists, and theologians. In one day, I can read quotes that inspire me, imagined thoughts of a toddler, a fake Bill Murray account (or is it *really* Bill Murray?), and ways I can fight for justice.

I follow some people who I completely disagree with because I think it's good to have a few opinions in my life that may not change how I think but may give me insight into why someone would think the way they do. Having a diverse social media timeline keeps me from feeling like I have permission to use "they," as if "they" aren't reading what I type. It makes me think twice about what I post. It makes me consider if what I post is hurtful or helpful. It has made me consider some of the ways I think about and see the world. It has made me think better and do better in the process.

I can enjoy live tweeting during award shows.

Social media is one of the best things to happen to award shows. As much as I would love to be able to not only attend an award show but also be backstage giggling with Beyoncé and Kelly Rowland about cupcakes, the next best thing is tweeting about the award shows with thousands of other people who are watching. I can dish about outfits, about how amazing a song is, about the hairstyle someone chose. I can be the fashion police, or I can be a thoughtful commentator. And I can do this without dressing up, going on a lemonade and raw oats diet, renting jewelry worth more than my annual salary, or smiling at people I don't like. It's the best!

I can be a fan.

Social media is way better than *Tiger Beat* or *Right On!* magazines could have ever been. Instead of having to cut out pictures of my favorite artists and bands and thumbtack them to my wall, I can follow these artists I love and every now and then communicate with them directly.

Dream Hampton, a pioneer hip-hop journalist and fabulous writer, followed me back on Twitter once, and I immediately felt famous. I tweeted to DJ Jazzy Jeff with a question, and he responded back. I called Brené Brown my cousin, and she tweeted me back and agreed. I can't wait to bring her to the next family reunion!

It's good to be a fan, to still have certain things or people whose work you admire. Being a fan keeps me from taking life or myself too seriously. It reminds me it's okay to be excited when someone's new album drops or when my favorite TV show finally releases a premiere date for the new season. Social media should be about having fun. It shouldn't just be about using our ALL CAPS to yell at each other and say things we would never say to someone's face.

This brings me to my next point.

CHAPTER 20

Reasons Why Social Media Is the Worst Thing That Ever Happened to Me

Being on social media is stressful. It can cause high blood pressure, panic attacks, and stink eye. Okay I have no medical evidence for this, but I do know if you let it, social media can ruin your life, your lunch, and possibly a few distant friendships.

Social media is Comparison Central.

In thirty minutes of scrolling through social media, I have wondered the following: Is my house clean enough? Is my relationship loving enough? Do I work enough? Do I work too much? We need to have kids right now! Never mind, kids are crazy—look what his kid did to the kitchen! I wish I had that couch. Do I get enough sleep? Do I sleep too much? I wish I had that house. I wish

I had that opportunity. How did she get to meet Jill Scott? I wanna meet Jill Scott. Why didn't I get invited to the movie premiere? Why didn't I get invited to the dinner party? I mean I probably wasn't gonna go anyway, but they could have at least invited me. Does she wake up looking that pretty? My hair never does that when I wake up. My #nofilter pictures never look like that. Did I choose the right angle for my selfie? Do I take too many selfies? Do I not take enough selfies? Should I do the selfie challenge? What about the love-your-spouse challenge? What about the gratitude challenge? Is it boot season? Is it sandal season? Is it cuffing season? Do I Netflix and chill? Do people who say Netflix and chill actually Netflix and chill? Is it crunk? Is it turnt? Is it lit? What is the age bracket for who should say what? Are my dinners foodie enough? Are my foodies dinner enough? Am I enough?

Before social media existed, I still compared myself to other people, still suffered with jealousy or envy. I just had fewer people and fewer instances to compare myself with. This is why studies show excessive time spent on social media can make us sad and depressed. But there have been no studies on how much of what we post and read there is actually true. How much of what's going wrong in our lives we hide with filters and camera angles.

I hate being added to random Facebook groups.

Whoever it is at Facebook that came up with the idea there should be no approval for being added to a Facebook group is my enemy. Being added to the "Isn't this funny" Facebook group, where the sole purpose of the group is to post jokes that aren't really funny, or the "I'm selling things you probably don't want" group or the "I'm selling things you probably don't want but I want you to sell these things as a part of my sales team" group, deserves a special kind of punishment. It is especially terrible when someone you know in real life adds you to one of these groups and you try to leave and they add you back in and then you try to leave again and they add you back in. This is what cusswords were invented for.

Social media drains my time and my feelings.

My grandma used to say an idle mind is the devil's workshop. I wanted to ask her what exactly does the devil have in his workshop, but I felt like that conversation wouldn't go well.

Do not scroll social media if you are bored, lonely, hungry, hangry, or tired; on Valentine's Day; during the "Aren't We So Disgustingly in Love?" thirty-day challenge; after a breakup; before a breakup; after fighting with your spouse; before fighting with your spouse; while potty training your children; when it's raining; when you've gained or lost weight; when you have a big project to finish; or when there is a dessert table nearby.

Do not scroll social media when you are trying to finish writing a book, or you will never finish writing your book. Do not scroll social media and call it research. Two hours later, you will know nothing more than you knew when you started and will have a craving for that chicken alfredo lasagna espresso smoothie because of some video you saw.

Social media can be a terrible soapbox and the worst pulpit.

Screens give us something to hide behind when we spew our ALL CAPS racist, sexist, ableist, xenophobic, homophobic, hateful comments. Social media means we don't have to look people in the eyes to see how our comments hurt their feelings. We don't have to think about how offensive our opinions are. We can step up to our soapbox without the bravery it takes to listen to anyone else, without the courage it takes to engage in the kind of conversation where we can learn something and possibly learn we are wrong.

Because of social media, I learn the offensive political beliefs of people I love. I learn the inherent sexism of church leaders I respected. I learn some of my friends don't eat donuts, cornbread, or cake. There is a lot of sadness in the world.

Social media isn't the best medium for conversations like these. It isn't the best place to disagree or to be understood. It can become a breeding ground for our pride, insecurity, and selfishness, and it can teach us to want to be right more than we want to love.

Social media sermons also don't preach well if our real life doesn't demonstrate the truth we say we live.

Sometimes I try to imagine what it would have been like if Jesus had social media. Would he have had a Facebook group for his disciples? Would Peter have live-tweeted the Sermon on the Mount? Would John have posted the fishes and the loaves on Instagram? Would Jesus' wine wedding miracle have had a hashtag? Would his mom ask him to post a picture of his miracle on Facebook for her? Would he try to unify the Android and Apple users?

I don't know. We'll never know. But I'm certain Jesus would use social media to do what he always does. He'd love those who so many people deemed unlovable. He'd invite the outcast. He'd have a low tolerance for those who hide behind their religious piety so they can seem like they are better than other people. He'd speak truth devoid of pride. He would still give his life for all of us: those of us stuck on our phones and tablets and those who prefer face-to-face to FaceTime. I'm also pretty sure Jesus would not invite anyone to play Candy Crush Saga.

Man, that last sentence was a good quote. I'll be right back. I have to go post that real quick.

CHAPTER 21

Failure

I hate failure. I don't care what all the business and leadership gurus say about the secret to failing well or how to fail forward or that failure is the secret to success. Let's have an honest talk about this. Failure sucks. Nobody likes to lose. Nobody sits in the middle of the shambles of their life and dreams about the article or book they will write one day about how they rose from the ashes of this moment like a phoenix or how they like to write things that are full of cliché.

Failure is what it feels like when no amount of counseling or forgiveness can save a marriage. When every attempt at good parenting still produces a kid who stumbles down a path that seems to lead to nothing but more bad decisions. When you sink your life savings into a business idea that never found its wings to fly in the ways you dreamed of. When you fail out of school. When you're fired. When you get laid off. When you break up, even though everyone thought you were the perfect couple. When you can't afford to keep the house, the car, the apartment. When you make a mistake so colossal that the debris of your bad decision wounds everyone around you.

I don't handle failure well. I am a recovering perfectionist. I am a classic oldest kid, trained to take care of everything and everyone. I am a church kid, raised to say and accept the good, convenient, Sunday school answers. I am Southern born and bred, trained to smile and be polite, even in the face of foolishness. The combination of these things makes me a prime candidate for holding my breath and holding it all together.

I was a good student, an overachiever. I liked school, and school liked me. Even though I haven't been in school in years, I still look at my life as if each season is a semester that I must pass. I plan excessively. I try to control my environment. I don't trust easily.

Failure isn't something that happens to "those people" or something we can avoid by being good. It is not a grade we get to skip. Life is not a class where each choice, decision, or mistake will hand us a pass or fail, an A for perfection or an E for effort. It is not something our privilege, our money, or our pride can protect us from. Like heartbreak, a bad hair day, or the flu, failure is coming for us all.

Failure doesn't want to be our assassin. It wants to teach us the hard things. The aftermath of when we fail is life's best X-ray. It tells us where we are broken, wounded, diseased. It tells us where we've been ignoring our hurt, our wants, our needs. It shows us who we are, who we've been, who we can be. Failure reminds us there is just as much strength in a beginning as there is in finding the ways to a new path when we've reached an unexpected ending.

Failure reminds us we're human; we cry, hurt, and bleed. Failure humbles us. It reminds us even our best-laid plans and organized attempts at controlling life's outcomes don't control much of anything. It is failure that teaches us the dangers of pride and the grace of surrender.

Jesus knows we are going to fail. He knows he will ask us to follow him and we will choose ourselves. He knows he will ask us to pray with him in Gethsemane and we will fall asleep. He knows he will invite us to join him at the table and we will say we love him and then betray him. He knows we won't always get it right.

God sent a perfect Son to take on all the failings of the entire world. He knew Jesus would get it right. He knew Jesus could take all of these failed human beings and make it so we could be called righteous. There is no rock bottom, no personal disaster, no amount of utter failure where Jesus doesn't walk with us.

Jesus invites the messed-up to dinner, to sit at his feet, to follow him, to know him, to be close to him, to be loved by him, to be forgiven, to grow, to be changed, to become more and more like him. Until we realize just because we've failed doesn't mean Jesus calls us Failure. Until we realize Jesus loves us with the kind of love that refuses to give up.

CHAPTER 22

Success

When I was a kid, I always thought success meant being rich. After watching Russell Simmons, Shawn "Jay-Z" Carter, and Sean "Puffy" Combs become the brand ambassadors for what it would mean to be a hip-hop mogul and watching Michael Jordan, Shaquille O'Neal, and Kobe Bryant become famous, wealthy athletes, it seemed like the road to success had to be paved with money. And gold chains. And TVs that rose out of the floor. And anything else I saw on *MTV Cribs*.

When I got to college, success became entangled with academia and the corporate ladder. So many of the students at my liberal arts school were vying for internships and grad school programs they hoped would propel them into careers. I didn't have a strong definition of success. I only knew I wanted to be a writer. All of the writers I admired were in their forties and fifties, and most of them hadn't seen any traction in their writing careers until their thirties. I had no definition of what success was supposed to be in my twenties.

I graduated from college months after September 11, 2001.

National security tightened; the economy was limping; and the job market was insecure. I applied to grad school mostly because I hoped it would buy me some time to figure out my life. When I wasn't accepted into any of the schools I applied to, I realized I had no contingency plan.

I spent my early twenties working temp jobs, performing poetry, and writing articles as an arts journalist. My temp job as a receptionist turned permanent, and it was the perfect job for a writer. I answered the phone and labeled envelopes for large mailings. I spent the rest of my forty-hour workweek writing poems, transcribing interviews for articles, and researching for my next query to a publication.

By the time I turned twenty-five, I longed for the stability many of my friends had been basking in since we graduated. Many of them had already bought their first home, had full benefits, got promotions, and even had employees who reported to them. Poetry and journalism paid sporadically, and when they did pay, it wasn't enough to live off of. So when a friend of mine suggested I apply for a writing job at a Fortune 500 company where she worked, I decided this was the most grown-up thing I could do.

After completing the interview process while recovering from surgery to remove my wisdom teeth, I was hired for the job. My résumé and demeanor must have outweighed my slurred speech and swollen jaw. My first weeks in a cubicle smelled like success. I had health insurance, a 401 (k) plan, and my own direct phone line. I had a supervisor, a manager, and coworkers. There was break time, lunchtime, and another break time. I wore a blazer and panty hose. I had work shoes. I thought I'd made it.

It seemed the way to success only meant I needed a ladder to climb, but after a few months, I realized there was nothing up the ladder I wanted. I wrote at my job but was expected not to be creative and not to ask a lot of questions. I discovered success for me was about doing something that challenged me, where I could work with words and use them in creative ways to make people think, make people laugh, help people learn. I knew the only way I'd be able to do that would be to work for myself.

I learned that a good paycheck, a cubicle, and benefits did not equal success. I started to wonder if maybe success had less to do with money and possessions and more to do with what I had to offer that could help the world and my community.

Success is not just a business suit and an office with a view. Success is not money or status or keeping up with the Kardashians or whoever is my personal version of the Joneses. Success is not fame or likes or YouTube views. Success isn't the same for everyone.

For some people, success is getting out of bed each morning and not letting depression keep them from facing the day. For some people, success is staying sober, one day at a time. For some people, success is choosing one cookie instead of six. For some people, success is not letting their background, economic status, or past mistakes dictate their future.

Sometimes I have feared success just as much as I have feared failing. Because I feared what people would think if I started my own business or pursued my dreams. It scared me to imagine a life where I was doing and not just dreaming. What if I do what God is calling me to do? What if it requires a lot of me? What if it's easier to talk about it than put action to the words I say? What if my pursuit of my dreams makes other people around me uncomfortable because they are fine being stagnant and not pursuing theirs? What if there is no one to hold me back except for me?

When I was eight, I played Scrabble with my Grandma Bert and her friend Ms. Mickey. I played the word *success* and spelled it s-u-c-e-s-s.

"You spelled *success* wrong," my grandma said.

"Oh, Bert, she's just a child," Ms. Mickey said.

"Take 'em up," my grandma said and started to pick up the tiles. "She got to learn."

Sometimes I still misspell success, assuming it must be spelled with financial wealth, social status, social media likes, or applause. Sometimes I need to examine my "tiles," the building blocks I use to create what defines success to me.

Now I know success is much more holistic than I imagined. I don't want to define success based on money, jewelry, or what I own. There are many people who have enough money where they don't have to worry about paying their bills but quickly discover money can't love them, take care of them when they are sick, give them peace, or help them rest.

Success is finding ways to serve and help my community. It is seeing what I have and the influence I'm given as resources to give and offer, not things to hoard for myself.

I interviewed one of my mentors and former pastor, Dr. Claudette Copeland, for my YouTube series Behind the Poetry. I told her how she'd taught me so much about the intersections of leadership and humility, boldness and understanding, caring for others and taking good care of yourself. I asked her what advice she would give to a roomful of young women leaders. Her answer applied to leaders regardless of gender or age.

"Be sure with all your aspirations that you love the people

right who love you right. Don't step over them or leave them behind in your ascent to your greatness. When you're in a hospital bed and you need somebody to hand you a glass of water, the stage won't be there. Love well and love right," she said.

Success is not just about the balance in my bank account or the status I can amass. Success is also about the state of my soul and the balance in my relationships. If I am kind and humble. If I can serve alongside others. If I can take whatever I'm given and leave it better than it was when I arrived.

Maybe I am most successful when I take my grandma's Scrabble advice and apply it to real life. No matter how old I am or how much I think I know, maybe success is realizing I've always got a lot to learn.

Part Five

Ctrl + Alt + Surrender

The Soundtrack

Pages of Life—
Chapters I and II

by

Fred Hammond

I have loved gospel music since I was a teenager. I sang in the choir most of high school, and my dad and stepmother directed the choir at their church when I visited during the summer. Gospel music taught me about harmony and the importance of the words *soprano*, *alto*, and *tenor*.

Fred Hammond's *Pages of Life* was released in 1998, the year I left home for my freshman year of college. It was the perfect antidote for homesickness and became the spiritual anthem of my college years.

I held on to the verses of Psalm 103 as Fred arranged them to a soulful, gospel groove. I thought about my grandma during Fred's 1990s rendition of the old hymn "Jesus Is All the World to Me." God and I had a lot of surrender conversations to "Please Don't Pass Me By," "Your Steps Are Ordered," and "No Weapon."

This album carried me through college, heartbreak, grief, transitioning into a new job, and preparing to get married. It has brought me to tears on road trips, in airplanes, and in a room all by myself. The songs here remind me that God always knows exactly what he's doing and that the hardest and best thing I can do is trust him.

CHAPTER 23

Soul and Body

Everything I knew about healing I learned in church. I grew up in a nondenominational church with Pentecostal sensibilities. There was holy oil. There was laying on of hands in prayer. Sometimes this prayer led to someone fainting for a few minutes. We referred to this as "slain in the Spirit." We danced to organ music fueled by quick drumming. We referred to that dance as "shouting" even if the person doing the dance wasn't shouting at all. I wondered why the shouting dance never looked like the Bankhead Bounce or the Running Man. I never got any answers on this.

If you were sick, you went to the altar so that pastors, elders, and ministers could pray with you. If you believed God, if the right prayer was prayed, you could walk away from the altar no longer sick. You could be healed instantaneously.

Right before my husband and I got married, I sat in a doctor's office and tried my best to cope with a negative diagnosis. Not life threatening, but concerning. Could be harmless but needed to be watched. My doctor rattled off numbers and alternatives for treatment. I didn't really process any of them. The words "something is wrong with me" filled my throat until I could hardly swallow.

Within the first year of our marriage, my could-be-harmless condition worsened. I was tired all the time and could barely make it through mundane tasks like grocery shopping without being in debilitating pain. My alternatives for treatment would be very invasive and would most likely not permanently solve the problem. I was staring down the barrel of a possible life of continual invasive treatments.

While we were exploring our options, I found a holistic naturopath who specialized in conditions like mine. Her consultant fee was a fraction of what we'd already spent in medical bills. The worst thing that could happen is I'd waste my time and a small amount of money. The best thing that could happen is she could actually help me get better.

She had a cheery demeanor, somewhere between that of a personal trainer and a morning person. I told her my symptoms and conditions. She asked for the results of any tests or scans I'd had. We reviewed them. She asked about my diet and made me list for her what I was typically eating for meals and snacks. She told me to stop eating most of what I called "healthy" and quite a few things that would drastically change what I called "dessert." She sent me an herbal plan that would help balance my body and decrease my pain.

Then she asked, "How are you? How is the rest of your life going?"

"The rest of my life is fine," I said.

At least it was fine until you told me I couldn't have brownies anymore, I wanted to say.

"Whatever happens in our bodies sometimes starts in our souls. So what's going on with you? How's your relationship with your husband?"

"My husband and I are doing great. We're in a really good place."

"How's your stress level?"

"I'm more stressed than I admit," I said.

"Why?"

"I have my own business, so a lot of the decisions for my career are on my shoulders."

"How did you grow up?"

"With my mom, grandma, and sister. My mom was a single parent, and so was my grandma. My mom worked hard to raise us. She struggled. She raised my sister and me in hopes we wouldn't have to struggle as much as she did."

"Your body is trying to tell you something. Sometimes when you have pent-up fears and stress, your body has a way of letting you know you need to slow down and take better care of yourself. You may have watched your mom struggle, but you are not your mom and your husband is not your dad. You have to let go of that fear now. You are safe."

Safe. Did she mean I don't have to strive? Did she mean I don't have to carry such heavy burdens on my shoulders as if Jesus hadn't already carried them all? Sickness and woundedness had robbed me so quickly of feeling safe, of remembering I am always safe with God.

"Focus on resting. Focus on drinking more water. Focus on asking for help where you are carrying too much stress."

Help. Did she mean I didn't have to do everything myself? Did she mean I should stop trying to fix, change, do? Had saying yes to too many things convinced me I was responsible for other people and things God never meant for me to be responsible for?

I used to believe God's healing was instantaneous. That prayers for healing were answered with a drive-through method. I pull up to the order window. I ask for healing. I pull up to the pickup window and receive my healing prepackaged in a box with fries and a drink. My body didn't need a quick fix. My body needed patience, care, love, and attentiveness. God doesn't just want to heal my body or take away my physical sickness. God cares about the sickness of my soul too.

Sometimes it takes weeks, months, years, and sometimes we spend the rest of our lives healing. Sometimes it takes surgery, chemo, an herbal regimen, and dietary changes. It takes time to untangle how the wounds from our soul affect the disease in our bodies. It takes time to wade through how our disease hands us wounds we carry deep in our souls. It takes time to learn how to take care of ourselves, how to slow down and rest.

Healing is hard, and sometimes it hurts, but in time, we walk better. We learn how to lean on God. We learn we're not strong enough. We learn we need help. We learn we can't control life as much as we'd like to.

Pain is no longer a part of my everyday life, but I've had to make a lot of changes to my lifestyle to help my body heal. I'm learning that sometimes healing means not just eating what is convenient, and it also means not pushing myself to the limits because that's what it seems like success is or means. I am constantly reminding myself I am safe with God. God is my healer. I matter to him—spirit, soul, *and* body.

CHAPTER 24

Needle Point

As a part of my continual healing process, I've been getting acupuncture, a weekly appointment to have needles placed on my
pressure points, a weekly commitment to take better care of myself.
My acupuncturist always asks me how I'm doing, and since she's
seen me nearly naked and knows my medical history, I tell her the
truth. Some weeks, I'm tired. Other times, I'm worried. Some days,
I'm dehydrated, and other days, I'm feeling peaceful and at rest.

"Don't worry," she says. "Drink your water. Get good sleep.
When it comes to healing the body, we will do the work we can
do, and we will trust God to do the rest."

She places needles into my skin, and the sting of the needle
goes away before I have time to think about how I might look
like a porcupine or Edward Scissorhands. She places me under a
heating lamp as if I am basking in the warmth until a server takes
me to a customer's table. She lowers the lights and says, "Have a
good rest." I always fight this idea. I talk trash to her in my mind.

*Girl, nobody is taking a rest. Acupuncture is not naptime. I'm
about to sit here and mentally go through my to-do list until you get*

back. I'm probably gonna go to the grocery store as soon as I leave here. I'm gonna get bananas and ground turkey and fresh basil and zzzzzzzzzzz . . .

I can hear my broken records in that alone time. God uses acupuncture to put a literal needle to my figurative records. Each appointment gives me the chance to hear the music my soul is making when I'm depressed, when I'm stressed, when I'm doing too much, when I'm not sleeping enough.

I can hear my soul more clearly when acupuncture puts those needles to my broken records. I hear that I am afraid, that healing never goes as quickly as I wish it would. That physical healing never happens without emotional and spiritual healing too. That I want to believe in the healer but sometimes he doesn't move fast enough for me. That sometimes the most productive thing I can do as I heal is rest. This seems so counterproductive for a doer and achiever like me.

When God lowers the lights and says, "Have a good rest," I fight him on this. I make lists of things I can do to fix myself, of ways I can help God, of ways I haven't been good enough or busy enough or smart enough or just plain enough. But when I take a listen to my broken records and decide to surrender to the God who can make the kind of music in me that speaks of grace and mercy, I realize I couldn't fix my broken records in the first place.

Our bodies do their best healing when we are asleep. Our souls do their best healing when we are resting in what God can do, not putting our confidence and trust in what our humanity and finite reach can do.

In what feels like ten minutes but has actually been fifty minutes, the acupuncturist returns, undims the lights, and removes each needle.

"Your body is responding well, Amena," she says. "See you next time."

After she closes the door, I sit on the edge of the acupuncture table, my mind returning to the life and plans waiting for me outside her door. I get dressed. I drive home in silence. Sometimes, on the way, I talk to God about all the broken records that have come to the surface in my latest appointment. Sometimes I realize I've been avoiding God because I want to do my own thing. Sometimes I realize I don't trust him as much as I wish I did. Sometimes I realize I am stressed-out because I say yes when I should say no and I do too many things on my own when I should ask for help.

The small sting of the needle combined with the force of stillness is teaching me to trust God above my own understanding, to acknowledge him and trust his direction, even when his direction is to stop or to be still. I'm learning that sometimes the most productive thing I can do is be still.

As God is teaching me, I pray for my soul to respond well and surrender.

CHAPTER 25

In Google
We Trust

I know when things are not going well with me based on the number of times in a week I find myself at the alluring blank box that is the Google search bar. That little search bar is so inviting. You can search via text, image, video, shopping, news. You used to be able to play some kind of lucky numbers there, but I haven't seen that in a while.

I've found instructions on how to flat twist my hair. How to make hair conditioner out of mayonnaise and avocado. I search Kelly Rowland's outfits. I look up pictures of Beyoncé to send to my friends to illustrate my points via text. Her pictures are more expressive than an emoji. I've self-diagnosed my stomach pain as some condition between gas and whooping cough. I have read countless Wikipedia pages as if they are inerrant fact. I've Googled "dogs with guilty faces," "what to do with a full tub of yogurt?," and "how to cook with dates." Not cooking *on* dates but cooking *with* dates, the fruit.

Google makes me feel like I'm somewhat solving my problems, because isn't research the first step toward a solution? When I need an answer, I sometimes go to God, but I almost always go to Google. My safety net when I'm stressed is Googling, planning, and worrying. Google always has an answer, even when that answer is buried in a message board, contained in a comment made by someone who most likely has no idea what they are talking about. God, on the other hand, is sometimes like the guy who's just not that into you but you keep waiting for him to call you back, and then when he does, he makes excuses about the ditch he has fallen into or that his pet fighter fish died, and that's why he hasn't had time to return your call.

I want answers! I want nebulous statements that pretend to be answers! I want bad advice from strangers! I have somehow come to believe that Internet searches and excessive information are my best way to survive in life. The results of this method usually show up in sleepless nights, failing health, and headaches.

Getting answers from God is a game of patience. I have had several conversations with God about why I don't think patience should be a part of the Christian journey. I haven't received a supportive response from God yet.

I trust Google more than I trust God.

But my trust in Google is temporary. Google has more information than I'll ever need about everything. It's quick, simple, easy. Even after I've read the seventeenth web page about how to sleep better at night, Google is terrible at helping me find true peace for my soul. As many links as Google can offer me on how to be more lovable, more kissable, or how to be a better wife or a better house guest, it can't show me how to find the kind of love that isn't dependent on my looks, mood, or status. Google can't tell me who I am. It can't pinpoint my identity for me. Only God can do that.

Sometimes God isn't about the quick answers and pat solutions. Sometimes God wants my connection to him to be more important than my comprehension of him and his ways. My life and identity can rest in God for eternity. The life and identity I find in a Google search could change minute by minute.

Trust is a tricky word. It makes me think of the corny trust falls I did during team-building sessions at my corporate job. It also makes me think of being tied to a railroad track while trusting that some hero is going to rescue me. This is how I imagine God wants my trusting relationship with him to be—me a centimeter away from danger, while he waits until the last second to save me. I don't trust that. Maybe that isn't what God is asking of me.

Maybe trust is less about God being some superhero who swoops in and saves the day just as I was about to give up. Maybe trust is more like the sigh of relief I take when I get home after a long day. Maybe it is more this assurance that I have a place where I am safe and loved, even when chaos is happening outside those doors or inside my soul. That place is in God, in trusting his plans for me, his love for me, his ability to take care of me and be concerned with both the details and the big picture of my life. Maybe God wants me to trust him even when I don't know how. Even when there are no easy answers. Even when there are no answers at all.

I like my understanding. My understanding makes sense and seems tangible. I continue to pray that God will teach me to trust him with all my heart. With my future. With my history. With my plans. When my plans fail. When I don't know and don't understand. When I'm scared and wounded and listless. I pray that I would see that blinking Google bar as an invitation to give all my trust to a God who can handle it.

CHAPTER 26

Janet Jackson and Control

I wrote a letter to Janet Jackson's fan club, sent her my fourth-grade school picture, and told her how much "Rhythm Nation" meant to me. I was a special kind of nerd.

It all started with her album *Control*. I listened to that cassette over and over again, and the words still ring in my head all these years later. Janet in the black jeans, crimped hair, large mic headset, dancing and singing. She made being brown and having hips and being soft-spoken okay.

My preteen self, who understood very little about the words I was singing, gave Janet some serious competition when I sang the song as loudly as I could in my bathroom mirror concerts. "Control" was about Janet letting the world and herself know that she was no doormat and would make her own choices about her life, a lesson I didn't fully understand or apply until I was in my mid-twenties.

All these years later, I still want control. I want to ride through life, hold it by the reins, and direct which way it goes. Like young Janet, I had to learn that part of life means choosing, not letting the opinions of other people override the voice of God and my own soul. But I also had to learn there would be many things in life I would not be able to control.

I can't control how long I have to stand in line and wait for things. I can't control other people's feelings or decisions. I can't use my calendar, alarms, and incessant planning to command the outcome of my life. The moment I start to act like a know-it-all is when I become more aware of how much I don't know at all.

I work hard to be an achiever. I strive for perfection as if it is an actual possibility. I have spent years trying very hard to be exactly what I imagine people expect of me, as if this will make them give me more likes, love, or respect. But I can't control what other people think about me. I can't dictate how my detailed plans will actually pan out. I don't get to decide every outcome of my life.

I'm learning when life starts to crumble, when all the crutches I've trusted give way, my best course of action is surrender. In theory, the word *surrender* brings images to my mind of Psalm 23, of still waters and bubbling brooks. In actuality, surrender makes me feel like I'm supposed to do absolutely *nothing* about the looming problem standing between me and a good night's sleep.

I'm not really good at letting go. I'm the best at holding on, even if it hurts my hands and knuckles, even if the person or thing or idea I'm holding on to isn't what's best for me. I keep a closed fist and a tight hold on most things because I've been left before and I'd rather hold on to something than have it leave me.

I've stayed in bad relationships, not because the relationship was a good thing, but because letting go of it would make me feel like a failure, like everyone else was getting to graduate and I was being held back, like I didn't try hard enough.

I live my life like I'm holding my breath sometimes, like if I hold myself in a small enough ball, I will survive whatever hard times come my way. I'm still learning that letting go is the way to freedom. Letting go means admitting I can't control it, fix it, achieve it. Surrendering means admitting to myself and to God that I need help.

Surrendering means I really do trust God to know and do what's best for me, more than I trust what I think I know or understand. As much as I want to hold on to things or people or ideas or plans, I have to make sure I put my trust in the One who made the people, who gives the ideas, who conceives all the plans.

Surrendering is not a one-time experience. It is something I must do every day, moment by moment. It is where I must learn how to rest. Not just the kind of rest we get when we sleep, but a rest we need in our souls, especially when we take all of the problems of life and carry them on our shoulders as if we have the strength to carry it all. There is only One who carried it all, whose shoulders are strong enough for any problem, disease, concern, worry, wound, or frustration. His shoulders are big enough to carry today and eternity. God is the one who truly is in control.

CHAPTER 27

Ministry of Disappointment

I thought I'd be pregnant by now.

Full stop. Hard return. I will sit a few minutes after writing that sentence. I want to highlight and delete. I want to press backspace, as if a button on my laptop can keep that sentence from being true. I imagined my mid-thirties differently. I thought my guest room would be a baby room. I thought I would have smiled at my baby shower by now, gentle hand on a round belly. I thought by this time, I'd have a calendar full of playdates and plenty of funny kid stories to tell.

Instead, it's just my husband and me. This isn't a bad thing. This is in fact enough. My husband and I are a family. Having a child doesn't start our family. These are the things I tell myself when people whose manners exist somewhere between well-meaning and none of your business search the torso of my shirts with their eyes, trying to discern if I am hiding a pregnant belly from them. These are the things I remind myself of when enduring conversations that start off as small talk and turn to the dangerous territory of statements that stab you right between your heart and your unanswered prayers.

"Are you pregnant yet? Are you trying?" they ask, followed by intrusive suggestions and weird home remedies. "Don't wait too long," they say, as if we are waiting this long because we want to. "Have you thought about adopting?" they say, followed by a story of a random couple who adopted a child and then surprisingly had a biological child. As if we haven't walked beside our friends as they journey in the honor of adoption, as if adoption is a consolation prize or busy work while we wait for the "real thing," as if adoption should only be plan B.

Mostly we smile. Nod. Change the subject. Sometimes we get angry and frustrated and not so polite. We don't tell anyone how these conversations make us cry when we are alone. How we hold our breath until the awkward conversation is over, until the dinner has finished and the plates have been wiped clean. We say less and less. We don't even make comments about the future children we dream to have. We realize we are too fragile for the pointed questions and the oversimplifications.

I ask myself all sorts of things. Does true womanhood really hinge on a woman's ability to become a mother? Why do I hold myself to this ticking biological clock and some ridiculous social media standard that says I should have children by now? Is my identity wrapped in checking off some arbitrary list of achievements? Does my life not matter if I am not married with kids, with a certain income bracket, with a house in a certain neighborhood, with a list of ways to describe my cool life to people I meet at parties?

Our journey to one day having children has not been blissful, innocent, joyous, or as easy as I expected it to be. It has been a journey of loss, heartbreak, delay, doctor appointments, test results, delays, stress, frustration, more appointments, more delays. Hope seems to be a liability too expensive to carry in the face of so much disappointment.

My relationship to God and my feelings about prayer became tumultuous. I found myself wincing in my faith, praying cautiously because I don't want to deal with asking God for something when I think he will disappoint me. How do I keep going to God and asking when it seems like his consistent answer is *no* or *wait*? How do I keep believing the God who says *no* or *wait* when he knows how much that *no* or *wait* hurts me? How do I believe that God actually has my best interests at heart?

I spent the first year of this journey saying things like, "We are not these people. We are not the people who watch all of our friends around us get pregnant and have babies while we have no idea when it will happen for us." I learned there is no such thing as "these people." We don't get to choose. Everyone carries a load; we don't get to say what load, how we'll carry it, when we'll get it, or how long it will last.

I grew up as a church teen in the 1990s. Kirk Franklin had just proved that gospel songs could be played in church and in the club. Gold and purple "Jesus Is Lord" banners were selling out as fast as you could sing a Maranatha song. It was an age of believing the gospel could be connected to prosperity, that in the name of Jesus we could not only find love and peace, but also Benzes, McMansions, future husbands (also known as Boaz), future wives (also known as Proverbs 31 women), land, larger paychecks, and awesome shoes. Whether you named it and claimed it or marched around it six times in silence and the seventh time while blasting your loud trumpet (or shofar or boom box or tambourine or whatever you had on hand), believing these things would bring you the answers to miraculous prayers became a way of life.

I don't mean to poke fun. Okay, I do a little bit, but I can't completely poke fun. Sometimes I watched those prayers work. I watched people of faith pray for the sick, and the sick were healed. I watched church members move into houses the lender had nearly laughed them out the door for attempting to buy. I watched Boazes and Proverbs 31 women find each other, marry, and have pretty babies. So for years, I assumed this was the walk of faith. You see something you want; you pray and ask God; and you quote God's Word that applies to said request. You focus your positive thinking on the fact that God is powerful enough to answer and that he will do all in his power and with his unlimited resources to fulfill your request.

Then I grew up. I am learning the painful truth that even when you pray and ask God, even when you quote back to God the applicable Scriptures, even when you walk around the object you are praying for six times and play your trumpet on the seventh, God doesn't always answer the way you want him to.

What do you assume about a God who does this? He must be mean, cold, distant, unloving, inconsiderate. He must be more human and less holy, right? He must care about other people more than he cares about you. He must not see how hard you've tried to be good/honest/righteous.

Sometimes God is the great leader in the ministry of your disappointment. Sometimes you don't get the job you prayed for. Sometimes the Boaz/Proverbs 31 woman you thought you were supposed to marry doesn't even want a second date. Sometimes you want a Benz and you can only afford a hoopty. Sometimes God allows you to be disappointed. Sometimes you learn through tears, heartache, anger, and frustration that God is not a yes person.

I didn't want to write this chapter this way. I wanted to have a happy sitcom ending for you. I wanted to be able to tell you this story from the lofty place of prayers answered. I wanted to be the heroine, the central character to this great baby romcom. I wanted to spend a short time telling you this hard time we had and spend most of the time telling you the amazing story of how that all changed. But I'm not there yet. I don't know when I will be. I don't know if I will be.

Some people said this would be a season, and maybe it is, but it hasn't ended yet. It's gone on longer than I thought I had the strength to walk. Sometimes I get so weary all I can muster in prayer is "God, help me." And sometimes no words come, and I trust he hears the things my soul wants to say when it hurts too much to gather the words to express.

Maybe you've heard enough heroine stories. Maybe you watched enough sitcoms to be sick of happy endings written too quickly. Maybe it's pride that makes me want to present to you a pretty picture, a perfect image of what I imagine God's faithfulness has to look like. As if God's faithfulness isn't also in these breaths I take every day, isn't also in the way my grandmother's voice goes up a few notes when I call to check on her, isn't also in the friends who pray with me and let me cuss and say highly inappropriate things and love me anyway, isn't also the redemption that can only come from Jesus, isn't in the way God's plans are always better than mine every time.

I'm learning to accept this mystery of God. There are many things about God I will come to know or understand, and there is plenty I will never know, never understand, never be able to put words to.

I wish I had answers for you. I wish we could play M.A.S.H. or flip over the eight ball and predict the future. One of the limits of humanity is knowing only exactly what we know right now, right where we are. One thing I want my soul to remember and I want your soul to know is that life isn't always good; humans aren't always good; but God is good. Always.

I don't say that because it's convenient, and I don't say it to silence your frustrations, doubts, and questions. I say it because our tears and frustrations and doubts and hurt feelings and anger matter to God. I say it because I know how scary hope can be when you've lived with disappointment so long. I say it because I'm living every day trying to hold the tension of fully trusting in a God my humanity will never completely understand. As I sit in that tension, my heart still wants to believe in the God whose love is found in prosperity and poverty, in answers and in questions, in disappointment and in miracles.

Part Six

Home

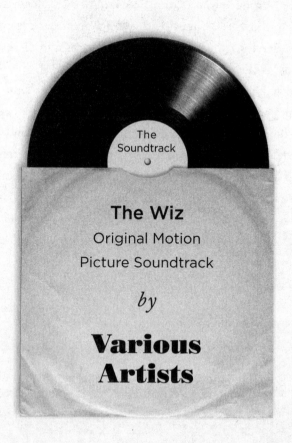

The Soundtrack

The Wiz
Original Motion
Picture Soundtrack

by

**Various
Artists**

 Kimberly's husband, Dedrick, loves *The Wiz*, and before living with them in my early twenties, I don't think I'd ever watched the whole movie. They had a Christmas tradition each year to watch *The Wiz*, so I joined mostly because I am always a fan of Michael Jackson's music.

Quincy Jones took the story of *The Wizard of Oz* and not only produced fantastic songs and beautiful orchestrations, but he helped produce one of the first large-scale, all-black-cast Broadway shows. The music provided a great backdrop for a story of searching for home in so many places and discovering that home is closer than we think.

When Dorothy, played by Diana Ross, sang "Can I Go On?" she put words to all of my aimless, confused, uncertain twentysomething feelings. Like Dorothy, I didn't know what I was made of or what I was afraid of. My favorite song from *The Wiz* is "Home." Just like Dorothy, I was searching for home too, looking for ways to find a heart, discover courage, and use my brain. Dorothy and I both discovered the journey home can be an adventure full of questions, song, and finding the right people to take that journey with you.

CHAPTER 28

Adventures in Staying

My husband and I sat next to each other at a lawyer's office to face a mountain of paperwork. We were buying our first home and felt like two kids wearing our parents' clothes, fishing our hands out of sleeves that seemed too long, getting ready to sign our lives away for the next thirty years.

This is the closest we had come to saying vows and making promises since our wedding day. Visions of the future danced behind our eyes. Would our future children know this house? Would their little feet lightly patter its floors? We imagined family gatherings, Thanksgivings, Christmases, birthdays, house parties. What would our family table be like?

My husband and I both changed addresses many times as kids. I grew up a military kid of divorced parents, and he grew up a pastor's son. The calling to serve our country or our God sent our parents packing and unpacking several times in our childhood. I cried over friendships lost, over school years that must be interrupted to face life in a new city.

I attended eight different schools between kindergarten and my senior year of high school. I spent most years dividing my time between summers with my dad, stepmother, sister, and two brothers in one state, and the school year with my mom and sister in another. I've lived at seventeen different addresses in my life. I'm prepared to pack luggage for any length of trip. I have mastered the art of travel-size toiletries.

I learned how to make friends anywhere and how to find something in common with almost anyone I meet. I lived on the West Coast, in the South, the Midwest, and Texas. I took my first flight at four years old, and I'm so comfortable flying that my white noise of choice mimics the sound of an airplane cabin.

I've never fantasized about living in Brazil. I never dreamed of Paris, London, Milan, Cairo, or Johannesburg. I fantasized about *home*. I always had a twinge of jealousy for my friends whose parents lived in the same house all the years they grew up, whose parents still have the same phone number, same candy dishes full of peppermints, same old wallpaper and family photos.

Which is why the idea of having a permanent address with our names on the title and deed is cause for pause and reflection. As my husband and I unpacked our life and left the boxes on the curb for the weekly trash run, learned how to newly navigate a city we have both called home for years from our new address, and stared at blank walls and rooms that are now canvas to us, I know a new calling.

I don't begrudge my childhood. I am thankful for the experience of having lived in different places, sat at different tables, learned to make friends, no matter what our class, culture, or skin color. This seemingly vagabond life prepared me for what I'm doing today: traveling, speaking, listening, performing, meeting new people from all walks of life and with all sorts of beliefs.

We have walked alongside many of our friends as faith and calling has led them to cross seas, sell possessions, uproot comfortability, serve in areas that are underserved, and immerse themselves in cultures very different from their own. Our journey has been different from theirs. As we unpacked our boxes and settled in, we realized we were beginning a new adventure with new focus.

God is calling us to an adventure in staying, a journey of finding and keeping home. As traveling artists, my husband and I will find ourselves in many hotel rooms, churches, venues, and tour buses, so we've learned to make home wherever we are. But God has also given two people who are well acquainted with boxes, moving trucks, and luggage a place to unpack, breathe, rest, get to know our neighbors, serve our city, and be a part of the art, creativity, and community that is being built here.

I don't long for a faraway adventure, although if one comes along, I'm happy to pack a bag and embrace the journey. I'm learning there are many times in life when God will call us to leave. But there are also times when God will call us to stay. The lesson isn't just in the staying or the leaving. The lesson is in continuing to follow the God who calls, whether it means we pack what little we have in a bag for a new address, or whether it means we unpack our life, put things in their respective drawers and cabinets, and make ourselves at home.

CHAPTER 29

Family Business

My dad sat next to me on the couch. It was the first time in my thirty-five years that we'd ever set a time to talk, just the two of us. I have been speaking in front of crowds since I was a kid, but that day, I was the most nervous I'd ever been, and there was no crowd at all.

It was my first trip back in years to the city my dad, stepmother, brothers, and extended family called home. Our family had recently been through a catastrophic storm of the emotional kind. Relationships were fractured. Issues we'd been avoiding for years had come to the surface, demanding to be addressed. I had a speaking engagement close by, so Matt and I decided to stay a couple of extra days in hopes that spending time with family would heal some of the wounds we were all experiencing. But I didn't want to leave without talking to my dad one-on-one.

There were questions I wanted to ask that only he could answer. There were things I needed to say for the sake of my own soul. He apologized for things. He told me he just wanted all of his kids to think well of him. He described the past ten years of his life—the struggles, the wounds, the lessons learned, the places of regret.

I looked at my dad and listened as the words he said seemed to affect the very rate at which my heart could beat. I saw his hurt. I saw where he was still trying to figure things out. I saw him not just as my father but also as a man, an imperfect human being trying to reconcile his mistakes and his choices.

Over the years, our relationship had left me with a peculiar set of feelings. Sadness for the time lost between us. Anger at the ways his absence had left me wondering about my own intrinsic worth and value. I loved the ways he could crack a joke or pack so much wit into a short phrase. I loved watching him play piano in his basement music room and how he gifted me with his love for music. All of these feelings sat right next to each other, just like he and I did that day.

"I wish we were closer," I said. "I wish we talked more, knew each other more."

"I'm glad we talked through all this. I feel like we can move forward from here," he said.

I didn't want the conversation to end. I scanned my brain for any other questions I could think to ask him.

"How can I pray for you?" I asked.

"Pray that I would find peace. I need some calm in my life," he said.

I thought later how peace and calm are two different things. Calm depends so much on our circumstances, but peace is a spiritual benefit that can only come from God and can exist even in the stormiest of circumstances.

For so long, I thought I wasn't good enough, smart enough, funny enough to find myself in the crosshairs of my dad's affection.

I thought maybe I was too emotional, too soft-spoken, too soft. Sitting down with my dad for that short amount of time matured me. Like six-year-old Amena finally got some answers to the questions that had left her little soul wounded.

I realized it wasn't my fault that my dad and I weren't close. It wasn't because of things I hadn't done enough of or too much of. It was the first time I realized my worth didn't have to rest in the closeness of our relationship. I didn't have to beat myself up anymore. I didn't have to strive. I no longer had anything to prove.

In our family, we are all walking our way into a new normal. My dad and I message each other from time to time. We talk about work and family. We touch base on holidays. I ask him questions about our family tree as I discover more of who I am through the stories about my great-grandparents and ancestors.

No easy answers here. Not a happy ending. But the more I live, the less I expect one. Happy endings are too convenient. They only belong in film or fictional stories. Real life is too adventurous and hard and beautiful to be reduced to neatly tied-up plotlines. In real life, woundedness and healing, grief and joy, doubt and gratitude sit closer than we think. I'm learning to sit in that tension, to find God waiting for me in the joy, in the tears, in the doubts, in the faith, in the questions.

CHAPTER 30

Warrior Women

When I was a little girl, my grandma watched two TV shows religiously: *The People's Court* and *The Young and the Restless*. The latter was referred to as her "stories" and should not be interrupted for conversation or emergency, unless it was a commercial break. During the commercials, my grandma would scold or applaud the characters, extracting life lessons on how Nikki and Victor's relationship wasn't working because they didn't "love one another like the Bible says."

I never scheduled my day around Judge Wapner or Mrs. Chancellor, but I found my own "stories" in *Grey's Anatomy*. I know the characters by name, and sometimes when they are in a tough spot, I'm tempted to pray for them, until I remember they are fictional characters. I'm a sucker for a hospital drama, so I jumped ship from watching *ER* when a young, hip hospital show began starring these new interns: Meredith, Cristina, Izzie, George, and Alex.

I chastised Meredith for sleeping with her boss. I felt her pain when she spoke the "Pick Me, Choose Me, Love Me" monologue in the scrub room. McDreamy, McSteamy, Burke, Bailey, the Chief, the on-call room, the break room, the operating room, the makeups, breakups, firing, hiring, and all the quintessential Shonda Rhimes's cliffhangers kept me glued to my couch.

Maybe my grandma was right. Maybe we can learn something from all the drama in our "stories." When I watched the season 10 finale and exit of one of my favorite *Grey's* characters, Cristina Yang, played by phenomenal actress Sandra Oh, I felt like I was saying good-bye to an old friend. In one of Cristina's final scenes with her best friend, Meredith, she said, "You're my person. I need you alive. You make me brave."

When I was a little girl, my mom and her best friend, Naima, used to stay up late, way past my bedtime, talking, laughing, and reminiscing. Their friendship has remained a steady pillar as their romantic relationships have come and gone and as their homes have slowly emptied of children to raise. They have walked each other through birth, loss, love, divorce, and job promotions. No matter how much their lives change, they always find themselves sitting across from each other discussing everything over a hot cup of tea. They are each other's person.

I learned from watching them how important it is for me to have women friends in my life who will help me to be brave, who will be my person. I've always leaned on a cadre of strong, funny, truthful, fabulous women. I envision us all strong warriors, fighting the good fight of faith, yoga, and chocolate; espousing to each other the good merits of biscuits, stillness, and dancing. Womanhood is a journey that is best walked together with other women. I'm thankful for so many warrior women who have walked this journey with me.

For my mom, who by the time she was my age was raising

two daughters by herself. Who worked her dream job and encouraged us to do the same. Who still takes my worried calls when I'm sick. Who prays for me and with me. Who is now my mom and my friend.

For my sister, Makeda, who is the best trash-talker I've ever met and refuses to make herself small for anyone, who helps me to silence the people-pleasing, critical voice that all too often runs rampant in my head. Who makes me laugh, cackle, and giggle. Who says so many things I think but am too afraid to say.

For my best friend Adrienne, who decided to be my friend in high school, despite the way I wore crew socks with my dresses. Who is one of the most hilarious people I know. Who when she says, "I'm proud of you," makes me feel like I can make it through just about anything. Who prayed for and with me and holds me to the truth of the gospel.

For Candi, and how the rhythm of our friendship is always on concentrate. We will cry, cuss, cackle, and keep it real before most conversations get past what the weather is that day.

For my best friend Kimberly, who let me live in her house when I was still trying to figure out what to do with my life, who taught me the importance of seasonal shoes and convinced me to wear clothes that actually fit me. For celebrating with me in the best of times and coming to my house and grieving with me in the worst of times.

For Kristen, who drove to see me perform while she was eight months pregnant. Who also came to a tour stop I had in her city and ironed my shirt and cried with me while I was still reeling from a miscarriage.

For Missi, who is not only my sister-in-law but also my friend, my frister. Whose kitchen has become the headquarters for many a real conversation. Our text messages are some of the realest things ever written. Who opened her home and her life to me, who shakes her booty with me in Zumba class, who understands the importance of a good donut.

For Nish, who has been known to accept a call from me crying. In the middle of the day. With very little ability to make sense of anything I'm feeling. Who didn't have advice or the right answers, but had a well-timed and well-articulated cussword to say in the way only she can say it.

For my girlfriends who are preachers, activists, writers, entrepreneurs, businesswomen, artists, whose leadership teaches me to fight for justice, drink my water, wear a bold lipstick, sleep, celebrate, lament and ask for help, pray even when I want to cry and cuss. Who remind me of my worth and value.

For my girlfriends who have struggled with disease, grief, and heartbreak. As I have watched many of them find joy and gratitude while walking through sorrow, I'm encouraged to be more joyful and grateful too.

There are too many women to name here. I could spend chapter upon chapter outlining the ways my girlfriends have taught me love, truth, grace, fashion, and leadership.

It is a fight to believe what God says about me, to love and accept the way God made me, to do what God called me to do, even when it's not convenient or easy or applauded. I don't fight that fight alone. I walk with a squad of women warriors I would be honored to enter any battle with.

Sometimes it takes us so long to realize we need people and needing people doesn't make us weak. Cristina and Meredith in *Grey's Anatomy* reminded me we can't be brave by ourselves. We need someone to be our person.

So find someone who can walk with you, cry and snot with you, pray with you, laugh with you, sit in silence with you, grieve with you, cuss with you, grab your shoulders and speak the truth to you until it hits you right where you need it. When discouragement and pity creep in, lean on your person, and let them help you be brave, in hopes that when they need it, you can help them be brave too.

CHAPTER 31

Church

I come from a long line of churchgoing people: bishops, reverends, musicians, preachers, music ministers, church mothers, and deacons. Even before I had a relationship with God for myself, I assumed God must be real. Otherwise, I couldn't reason why my great-grandma Sudie and the mothers of the church would gather in her living room to pray to him, why my grandma played and sang his songs, why my mom woke up in the morning and the first thing on her agenda was to listen to recordings of his Scripture.

My family taught me that church was a place you went to, not because there was a show to see or there was a particularly good singer that Sunday. You went to remind your soul that God is bigger than you, that there are things about God you'll never understand. Church was a place to cry out, to moan, to laugh, to dance, to remember, to speak the future into existence. I would eventually have to find a relationship to God and to church for myself and learn from all the lessons church would teach me along the way.

Church of Origin

When I became a believer in Jesus as a teenager, the church my mom joined after recommitting her life to Jesus had a sense of formality. The women wore panty hose and slips under their dresses and skirts. The men wore suits and ties. Every leader, both men and women, proudly wore the title of deacon, missionary, minister, and elder. There was Communion on first Sunday, youth Sunday on fourth Sunday. There was a hymn of the month. A choir stand, choir director, horn section, a pianist and an organist, liturgical dancers, step team. (What can I say? It was the 1990s.) There was an offering, sometimes two. The choir sang a pre-sermonic song before one of our pastors or elders preached the sermon.

I learned the power of the Spirit of God. I learned to answer God when he called me. I learned to believe that God can change circumstances and people. That God can heal the sick and the wounded. To let God have his way, even if it meant the service ran long.

Church of My Twenties

The church of my college and early twentysomething years had very few titles. We called just about everyone except the pastor and his wife by their first names. We were young, and we wanted to find fresh ways to do church, so we eschewed a lot of the tradition we'd grown up with. We figured tradition wouldn't draw people who may not be Christian. We kept our church service succinct, our song selection intentional. We left no pauses or awkward moments in the service. We trusted the Spirit of God could move through the plans we made.

I began to question my Church of Origin, the whooping and hollering of the Pentecostal preacher, the belief that giving an offering could ensure one's blessings, the idea that I had to tarry to hear from God.

By the time I was twenty-five, the Church of My Twenties imploded. Terrible things were said. Wrong things were done and never addressed. It became an unhealthy place with unhealthy practices, so I left for the safety of my soul and my relationship with Jesus. I spent several months not going to church at all, wading through the church leadership voices I had let influence so many of my life's decisions, trying desperately to hear the voice of God.

Church had hurt and wounded me. Church had disappointed me. Church had made me lose some of my naivete. I didn't want to leave Jesus, but I wasn't too keen on his church, and I wasn't so sure it was worth it to put my soul and heart at risk by being there.

Church in Unlikely Places

I went back to the arts scene I had begun to avoid while I was so busy doing church work. I found God in a lot of unlikely places. I learned to see the beauty of God in art galleries. I learned to listen and be humble by attending open mics. I discovered the freedom of God on a dance floor.

I decided to try church on Sundays again, but this time, I picked a church too big for me to be noticed or missed. I needed a place where I could hide while my church wounds were healing. I cried through almost every service. I said I wouldn't. I promised myself I wouldn't cry. One Sunday, it was a song. The next Sunday, it was baptism, and the Sunday after that, it was the sermon.

After a few months, I joined a small group there. I spent the next two years studying the Bible and walking through life with those women. I learned about grace for what felt like the first time. I didn't always make it to church on Sunday, but I did my best not to miss our group meetings. I learned God was more interested in my being with him than in what I could do for him. I learned I wasn't valuable to God just because of my gifts or talents or ability to do. I learned my value came from Jesus and not my career or looks or connections or amount of cool.

Over the next few years, I was a part of two small groups like this. We walked each other through dating, marriage, breakups, promotions, career changes. I learned that church is so much more than a couple of songs and a sermon on Sunday. Church was also those women I told my mistakes and misgivings to, how we prayed for and with each other, how we pointed each other back to this sacred, ancient, yet always relevant text, how we reminded each other of our lifelong commitment to follow Jesus.

Church of My First Year of Marriage

When I started dating my then-boyfriend-now-husband, he had been a youth pastor for two years at a small church southeast of Atlanta. When I realized we were probably going to marry each other, I felt a small amount of panic about my relationship to church. I realized my lack of Sunday attendance wouldn't fly as the future wife of a youth pastor.

After we got married, I wasn't sure what the church's expectations would be of me as the wife of a member of the pastoral staff. I panicked at being saddled with the expectations I had done such a good job of walking away from. I lived in that tension for the first year of our marriage, as my husband and I juggled our respective roles of youth leader and traveling performer.

There were some good and grounding things to our time at this church. It kept us humble because, no matter how much our talents were applauded at some out-of-town stage, we returned home to a church body that loved us but wasn't enamored with the work we did. We came home to hosting events for students, meeting with parents of our youth, my husband doing hospital and jail visits while I attended women's Bible study.

I watched my husband create cool experiences for the students out of the bare-bones budget he was given. I watched how every staff member worked more than the one job they were paid to do. How the church was small enough for people to miss you when you were gone. I learned to love the people there and learned to let them love me. They surrounded us with so much love and time and gifts for our wedding. Many of them prayed for us and supported our time on the road. I lived in the tension of not wanting to find myself church-busy and losing focus on God while also wanting to support my husband's work in our church community. This tension never went away.

Church Reconnection

Right before our first anniversary, my husband's youth pastor job ended. By the time we bought our first home a year later, we found ourselves longing for church community, missing the experience of knowing and being known. We wanted to find a church in our neighborhood. We didn't want to commute to our church while driving past so many churches that were serving in our area. So we visited churches. Conservative, liberal, liturgical, and charismatic. Services that were barely long enough to sit down and services that lasted so long we wished we'd packed a lunch.

A friend of ours told us about a small church plant near our neighborhood and introduced us to the pastor. Service was long enough to sit down but not so long that it left me with regrets. The church took weekly Communion and sang the Doxology every week, along with a mix of soulful, traditional, and contemporary songs about God. The pastor preached while giving cultural and historical context to the stories, texts, and principles in the Bible. We have found a sense of home there.

Sometimes church still makes me panic. When a person or a thing wounds us, the soul forgives but the body rarely forgets—our bodies and the church body. Our bodies remind us of what made us afraid before, of the signs that should make us run. Sometimes I need to be reminded I am safe now. I may have been hurt before, but that isn't the only story I will ever live.

Today, church for me is a combination of the many church experiences I've had. It is a place that always holds the tensions of so many things. Church is a place that has wounded me, but it is also a place where I have found great healing.

As I get older, I find myself returning to the tradition of my Church of Origin. I sometimes long for the songs and hymns I learned as a kid, and I believe that God still performs miracles.

I still keep some of the enthusiasm of the Church of My Twenties, believing that Jesus followers, as the church we were meant to be, can really change our neighborhoods, cities, nation, and the world. I go to church some Sundays, but I know now that church community doesn't end there.

God still meets me in the Church of Unlikely Places: coffee shop conversations, soul music concerts, family dinners, unplanned times of quiet or silence. I'm learning maybe these unlikely places are where I am more likely to connect with God than I thought.

When I think of the Church of My First Year of Marriage, I remember watching my husband and the church staff walk with people through marriage, divorce, birth, death, sickness, and celebration. I know now being part of church community sometimes means walking the long road with people, and doing the work to make sure I am healthy and the church body is healthy too.

Now, my Church of Reconnection is starting to feel more like a place to remember; to grieve; to be reminded of joy; to focus on the cross, the crucifixion, the resurrection; to remember Jesus knows what it's like to suffer and he knows what it's like to heal. Church is becoming a place to live with other people while we all grow and change and are challenged. A place where I don't have to hide or tuck away when I want to panic or run, a space where I can be honest when I'm afraid or unsure or uncomfortable. Church will never be perfect, because its people aren't. But it can be healthy in its imperfection. It can be what Jesus intended. And I can be who Jesus intended too.

CHAPTER 32

Roots

I held my passport in my hand, still shiny and nearly brand-new. I'd only garnered two stamps from trips to Canada and the Dominican Republic. This time I was crossing larger seas into a continent I imagined would be a place of great tension and conflict for me.

For years, I had said no to opportunities to travel to Africa. In particular, if I was invited on a mission trip that seemed to be focused on poor Africans being helped by middle-class or wealthy Americans. In particular, if there seemed to be a dissonance between the concern for poor Africans and the concern for poor African Americans.

I didn't want my first trip to Africa to be riddled with viewing her as a place that needs assistance, as a place to visit because pity disguised as problem solving seemed like a good, Christian, American thing to do. The history of my ancestors was there in that soil. The woundedness of the bloodline of a people whose language and culture and customs were stolen from them was still waiting at the bottom of a Middle Passage sea.

I wanted my first trip to Africa to honor the ancestors whose names I would never know. I wanted to mourn the continent they were stolen from while basking in the joy of the rich cultures still thriving there.

I met Dr. Una Mulale at a women's conference where we were speaking. Her hair was twisted into a beautiful coif, and her hips were wrapped in bright and beautiful fabric from her native Botswana. I told her I loved her outfit, and we exchanged a few pleasantries. I was even more impressed when she took the stage to discuss the nation where she was born and raised and how God was using her medical degree and education in global health to improve the conditions for children in Botswana's hospitals.

We met again at another women's conference the next year, and she asked me to step into her office at an after-party, which basically meant occupying a vacant corner and talking through an idea she had going. She and her best friend, Leah, had cofounded Barona Children's Foundation, an organization created to establish Botswana's first Pediatric Intensive Care Unit and children's hospital.

"I want you to come to Botswana," she said. "I am hosting a Gratitude Gala there for medical professionals. I want you to come and share some poetry, and I want your husband to deejay," she said.

I ran through my usual Africa trip checklist: Does this make me feel uncomfortable or sick to my stomach or like Africans will be treated as less than? I felt none of those things, only the pride Una had in her country and in her people. Four months later, my husband and I were on a plane to Botswana.

We met Una and Leah in Maun, a medium-sized city in Botswana. There we met Bonty Botumile, a storyteller and community activist who converted her property to an arts center for young people to create, find their purpose, and build community. We learned about Love Botswana, an outreach mission founded by Jerry and Jana Lackey. We toured the Village Church where the Lackeys pastored and where the Gratitude Gala would be held. Jana took us to the Okavango International School, where we spent time with students from Botswana and many other countries. We visited Love Botswana's home for children who had been abandoned or had special needs.

We went on a horseback safari at the Royal Tree Lodge, where the giraffe made it very clear to us we were in their territory, not the other way around. We saw herds of zebra, impala, and gazelle. We saw flocks of ostrich. We went to sleep and sometimes stayed awake at the lodge where we were staying, listening to the noise of the mammals and birds around us.

At the gala, dignitaries sat next to common folk, chiefs sat next to nurses, while Una and Leah watched their dream of bringing the community together to build better medical care for Botswana's children become reality. After the gala, we traveled to the Okavango Delta for Leah's wedding. The only way to travel to the lodge where she would be married was via a tiny plane that could only seat six people, including the pilot. I may or may not have sung "In the Name of Jesus (We Have the Victory)" over and over until we landed.

When we arrived, the staff at the lodge sang a traditional Botswana welcome song. Shortly after sunset, Leah and her husband said their vows under a beautifully dark and romantic Botswana sky and spent their first few moments as a married couple being celebrated with the singing and dancing of the lodge staff and their friends from Botswana. I held Matt's hand, thankful for the adventure of our marriage and all the adventures our marriage had brought us, including rejoicing in a newly married couple's wedding vows underneath a sparkling lattice of stars.

The day after the wedding, we said good-bye to Leah and her new husband, and six of us rode seven hours to Francistown, Una's village, in an uncomfortable van with our knees in our chest. It was easy to forget about our rough travels after nearly the entire village greeted us when we arrived.

We met the village chief and Una's dad, uncles, aunts, and community. They prepared food for us, and we prayed and ate together. They asked us about America, and we asked them about Botswana.

"It honors us that Una wants to bring her friends home to meet us. We are Una's roots," her uncle said.

I took pictures of the older women in Una's village, their shawls wrapped around their shoulders and tied with a pin or brooch not unlike the ones my grandmother and great-aunts would have worn. Somehow, we were all inexplicably tied together, even after centuries and miles of distance.

Una had given us the opportunity to see Botswana as more than a two-dimensional representation of the faux African accents found in American movies or the "savage" narrative that pervaded America in an attempt to make slavery and racism acceptable. I experienced Botswana through the dance, music, strength, and stories of her people.

A year later, I traveled to Rwanda with women from the IF:Gathering and Africa New Life. Of a group of more than thirty women from America, I was the only black woman on the trip. I was nervous. During the week and a half we were in

Rwanda, there were repeated incidents of violence, police brutality, and racism in America. With little Internet access, I was unable to drown myself in the news and in my Facebook newsfeed. I was unable to console my friends who were heartbroken by all that was happening, but I was also better able to be present with the things I was learning in Rwanda.

The tensions of systemic racism that boiled over in America were a tough burden to bear while walking through a country that had been sliced open by the fear of its people—fear that caused neighbor to murder neighbor, friend to murder friend, relative to murder relative; fear that had produced one of the worst genocides in history.

I walked through the Kigali Genocide Memorial with Rwandan poet Michaela. I saw how the ravaging wounds of colonization brewed a division among the Rwandan people, how corrupt government and religion collided to cost the country the lives of so many citizens. My chest tightened at the pictures of babies, aunts, uncles, family members who had been killed. I read about genocides all over the world. I thought of my own country's sordid history of genocide, racism, and slavery; how fear, ignorance, and unfounded assumptions of supremacy led people to rape, enslave, and murder.

The memorial left a caution in my heart, to watch how far my fears can take me away from love and from seeing other people as creations made in the image of God. That night, the Africa New Life children's choir and dance team performed traditional Rwandan song and dance for us, and for the first time since I had arrived in Rwanda, I cried. I wept for the wounds in my own heart and in my own country. I wept for the places where my joy as a black girl had been lost. I wept seeing the freedom in the eyes of each boy and girl, how the light in their eyes gave me hope for how much freedom was truly possible. I wept at how God can take a wounded place and begin to heal there, even when that process is not quick and is not without its flaws and imperfections.

Later that week, I was asked to speak to a room full of Rwandan young women who were high school students at one of Africa New Life's boarding schools. I shared poetry with them; I told them about my mom, grandma, and sister and why they were my own personal sheroes. One of the young women asked me where in Africa I was from. I tried to be present with the pang in my chest while I explained to her that I, like most African Americans, didn't know my African country of origin because no records were kept of which country and village Africans were taken from during the slave trade; there is no record of the languages, customs, and cultures lost.

"You are Rwandan," she said, and the other students smiled and nodded in agreement.

Even though I was pretty sure there was no way that my being Rwandan was historically possible, my heart heard, "You are home."

When we returned to the guesthouse where we were staying, one of the American women on our trip came up to me to ask how I was enjoying the trip so far.

"It's been really beautiful and really hard," I said. "It's difficult being the only black woman from America on our trip, but it's been beautiful to meet and get to know the people here."

"It hurt my heart to hear you say you don't know where your ancestors come from," she said. "Have you ever thought about taking a DNA test to find out?"

"I have. I'm hoping someday I can complete a DNA test and add that information to my family tree."

I had thought about it many times. After watching the new version of *Roots* released by the History Channel, I had started tracing my ancestry. I was able to make it back to my fourth great-grandparents on both sides of my family, most of whom were enslaved. Between the documents on the ancestry site and interviewing my parents and grandma, I had learned about my sharecropping great-grandparents, about the church furniture my great-grandfather and his sons built in their small North Carolina town. I saw the marriage certificates of my second great-grandparents, and through the census, I learned how they took in extended family members during Reconstruction. I learned that some of my third and fourth great-grandparents were free before the Emancipation Proclamation.

Before that, the paperwork trail on them gets lost. I either find no information or I find a slave schedule, a census document where slave owners accounted for their slaves as property, where they are only listed as Negro, male/female, and their age. It is a certain kind of heartbreak to know at some point my ancestors were nameless and not considered to be people, that they were only their race, gender, and age. I know now why saying names and pronouncing them correctly is so important, because at a certain point, the names of my ancestors didn't matter. One of the last steps left for my family tree was to take a DNA test and find out where in Africa my ancestors were from.

"I hope I'm not out of bounds, but I'd like to pay for your DNA test," she said.

The next day, she and I sat in front of her laptop, browsing around on an ancestry site as she paid for my DNA test. After the confirmation went through, she turned to me and said, "I'm sorry for what my ancestors did to your ancestors. I know this is small, and it doesn't change or make that better, but it's one thing I can do, and I want to do it."

I didn't really know what to say. I'm so used to saying the equivalent of "it's okay" in conversations like this. I'm so used to stuffing down the hurt and woundedness and loss I sometimes feel when I think about the roots of my ancestry. So used to shrugging my shoulders as if it's not a big deal when it is. But that day, I sat with her words a few moments, I took in an apology that was too big for one person to truly give, but a necessary apology and acknowledgment nonetheless.

The DNA test and I arrived home at the same time. And I stared at it for three days. It seemed so simple, so clear-cut—putting my saliva in a vial and sending it off to find out the origins of my ancestry. But the presence of the test brought up some feelings of not belonging and of searching for home while still feeling lost that I hadn't been prepared to deal with. What would I discover? What family secrets might come to light? What would I do once I couldn't unknow the truth?

To me, a DNA test is usually used to settle a question of paternity. My dad and I have almost the exact same face, so I have no questions there, but this DNA test did feel like waiting for Africa and possibly Europe and possibly Native American ancestry to tell me if I belonged to them, and what if somehow the test came back and I didn't belong with anyone?

I did the one thing I do when I'm scared: I called my bold and sassy baby sister. I call her when I'm afraid because I know she'll hear me out, even if what I'm describing to her sounds absolutely crazy. I also call her because after she hears me out, I know that, if my fear is standing between me and something I should do, she will say a cussword to me in love, ask me why I'm letting fear stop me, and then tell me I can do this. I can face it. I can be brave. And then she'll probably take me to get my nails done, because that always helps me feel less afraid.

"You still haven't done the DNA test, my sister?" she said. "Why?"

"I'm not sure," I said, staring at the test.

"Are you scared of what it might say?" she asked.

"Maybe. I'm in my feelings. I'm feeling the lostness of having certain parts of my family tree I know nothing about. Feeling the weirdness of spitting into this tube and not knowing what the results will be."

"That's understandable," she said. "Send it off, my sister. When you're ready."

A couple of days later, I finally read the instructions and sent the DNA test out to be analyzed. Several weeks later, on a Friday night, my DNA test results arrived, and I stayed up half the night looking over them. Eighty-five percent African heritage, mostly from Benin and Togo, some from Nigeria, and some from southeastern Africa right in the region where Botswana is. No Native American ancestry, despite what my great-grandfather's family believed about his mother with the high cheekbones and ropey braided hair. Little to no English or Irish ancestry. Only 11 percent European, and most of that was from Norway and Scandinavia.

I looked at the pictures of some other people who shared DNA with me. I researched these African countries and almost immediately wanted to search flights to go there and meet my long long long long lost relatives.

I have traveled outside of the United States four times: Canada, Dominican Republic, Botswana, and Rwanda. In three out of the four countries, I was confused for a native, in each place having people walk up to me speaking their native tongue and looking back at me in confusion as they heard my American English. I could not return their Spanish, Setswana, or Kinyarwanda. They were trying to welcome me to a home I didn't know I had.

I still search for home in Africa, wondering what the villages were like where my ancestors lived before they were taken and brought to America. Wondering who was separated from whom. Was it mother from daughter? Husband from wife? What is my tribe like? Would I be able to make more sense of myself by knowing them?

My roots are full of hard things, sadness, loss, trauma, grief. The roots of nations and of families are not that different. They are both difficult to wade through, and it can be so challenging to see the strength as well as the weaknesses, the brave choices as well as the cowardly ones. But all those roots make me who I am, and I want to honor that with who I grow to be.

CHAPTER 33

Go Ahead and Get Happy

It was the night of the book release event for my first book, *Breaking Old Rhythms*. A few hours afterward. My husband and I were both dog-tired, which seems to be the hardest-hitting version of tired, at least from what I can tell from the cliché context clues. He slept peacefully, and being not only the band, deejay, and emcee but also the man who carried every last box, book, and piece of luggage for all the gigs we'd had the previous couple of weeks, he deserved his sleep.

I did not sleep. My mind pushed rewind and replayed the events of the evening while I watched intently, looking for a place I missed it, a mistake I made. I searched the eyes of my good friends who came to see us perform that night, looking for that flatness in their eyes that might say it wasn't quite good enough.

When people came up to me to say they enjoyed the show, to say they were looking forward to reading the book, a part of me kept wondering if they were lying to me. If maybe they were telling me these things because they didn't want to hurt my feelings by saying all of the things I could have done better.

This made me wonder, *Why can't I just be happy sometimes? Why is my good never good enough to me? Why am I always looking for a way to raise my already unrealistic expectations for myself? What's up with that?*

I am a realist, also known as a pessimist. My worst-case scenarios dress themselves as reality, so I listen to them. I married an optimist. I fell in love with a man who can find a sunny disposition in a thunderstorm cloud of circumstances, and this has been God's way of building my character.

Matt and I work together, create together, walk through messes and successes together. At our lowest points, I have been fraught with worry and fear. Matt will join me there for a few minutes, and then he will make a joke, do a dance, or offer to pick up donuts.

At our highest points, I have been nitpicky about all of the details that could have gone better and will mentally move on to the next thing without taking the proper amount of time to revel in a present good moment. He will laugh, smile until his cheeks hurt, and suggest we do something to celebrate until I have no choice but to give in.

Having Matt in my life is teaching me to go ahead and get happy. To remind myself that although I've experienced plenty of heartbreak and am just a human being with flaws and imperfections, that doesn't make me unworthy of love or good things.

I don't know if that little girl of divorced parents needs permission to go ahead and get happy or what. I don't know if all the years I spent trying to integrate myself into the lives of people I wanted to love me made me feel like there was some bar just a couple of feet shy of my reach that I would never be able to meet.

Experiencing hard times is the lot of every human being, but this doesn't mean I can't shush my realist/pessimist brain when necessary and enjoy the good times when they come. Life will bring plenty of hurts, but I will also experience many great firsts, opportunities to laugh and smile until my cheeks hurt.

Just because I'm a full-fledged grown adult doesn't mean I don't need God to be my parent, to show me I'm okay, to prove to me I don't have to keep chasing this unrealistic bar, to show me he's proud of me, pleased with me, to depend on him to teach me how to simply be myself and be content with that.

So before I critique myself or other people, I'm learning to take the time to be thankful, to say, "Thanks God; I made it." To say thank you to this amazing Jesus I've given my life to. I don't have to try so hard to be an insider. I don't have to press my cheeks up against the window of the cool kids' table or of someone else's family or home.

I have home with God in conversations with friends, in the love of family, and in my own soul. When I remember this, I feel less of a need to prove myself. I can finally stop trying to figure out what's wrong with me and just live, love, and enjoy being loved.

God, help me lean on your grace and learn to go ahead and get happy.

Part Seven

Searching for the Groove

The Soundtrack

A Seat at the Table

by

Solange

I wrote a lot of this book while listening to this album. Released in 2016, *A Seat at the Table* is a black girl love letter to herself—to take care of herself, to love herself, to stop trying to prove she's worthy, to accept herself just as she is. This album is about healing, about what to do with weariness, racism, and anger. With minimalist production and tender vocals, coupled with the storytelling of hip-hop artist and mogul Master P, and her own parents, Matthew Knowles and Tina Knowles Lawson, Solange created an album that must be listened to in its entirety.

Solange reminds me I have been more tired, hurt, and full of rage than I let on sometimes. Her songs remind me that just because I'm used to carrying a burden doesn't mean it's mine to carry. She sings of freedom, of anger to express but not internalize, of injustice, of pausing to ask questions even if the answers are not easily found. She reminds me of the importance of not just gaining a seat at someone else's table, but about building something of my own that provides a seat for other people too.

CHAPTER 34

Vinyl Destinations

A few years ago, I found myself searching the dusty aisles of thrift stores for old records, and I didn't even have a record player. Vinyl was making a comeback. Music listeners enjoyed the convenience of downloading but longed for the nostalgia of the vinyl record. The LP, too big to put in your pocket, with no way to record over it, stood the test of time. Vinyl wasn't just about the music; it was also about art, with meticulously designed covers and inside jackets.

In my first apartment, I created a wall of framed album covers to remind me of the artists who inspired me, to remind me it's possible to make art that isn't disposable. To remind me of the wonderful legacy of how albums and CDs were sold and shared and exchanged. When I picked up an album in a thrift store that looked a little worn on the corners, it reminded me that someone had loved that album once, had listened to it countless times.

For a while, it seemed the resurgence of vinyl belonged to deejays or to the hipsters who were rocking nineteenth-century beards and handlebar moustaches, cuffed skinny jeans, and Members Only jackets—the guys brewing their own beers and roasting their own coffee beans—but once again vinyl has gone mainstream. Barnes & Noble and Urban Outfitters are selling vinyl and record players. Music fans are longing to listen to an album from beginning to end, wanting to let the music breathe, to hear notes, lyrics, and metaphors as if for the first time.

When my deejay husband and I moved into our first house, we decided we wanted our front room to be a listening room. No television—just chairs, framed album covers and art on the wall, a record player and speakers.

Once every few weeks, we visit our favorite record store, Sunbrimmer, owned by a record aficionado named Mike. We thumb through rock, soul, funk, comedy, and soundtracks. His record store is like a fashion-forward boutique where the fashions rotate out before you can buy them up, except instead of racks full of polyester and leather, Mike specializes in one material: vinyl.

We've brought home Parliament, Rufus and Chaka Khan, The Jacksons, an entire record of directions on how to listen, and Whoopi Goldberg's Broadway show recording. We study the art on the cover and the inside jacket. We fill our house with the rich sound of analog. We like that the music doesn't play for hours, that at some point you reach the inevitable silence waiting for you when the record is done or needs to be turned over to the B side. Listening to vinyl makes us slow down, gives us ears to listen to an album not for its singles but for its concept, as an art piece, as a whole.

There are many words I grew up knowing, being born around

the same time as hip-hop: dope, fresh, cool, crib, homeboy, B-girl, and some others that probably shouldn't be named here. My parents grew up in the 1960s and 1970s, so I learned a few words from them: soul, funk, dynamite, and groove.

Whenever I hear the word *groove*, I think of what my mom's hips would do when Cameo came on the radio. I think of what happened at family reunions when our deejay cousin played "Brick House." It's hard to escape the groove. It's the rhythm guitar in "Dancing Machine," the bass line to "Let's Groove," the timbre of Frankie Beverly's voice in "Before I Let Go." I've always thought of the groove as what gives music soul, what makes you dance, clap your hands, and sing the lyrics too loud.

I started to study these large, round discs that had provided so many generations with music to listen to in their homes. There is a lot more we can gather from records than music and cool cover art. The resurgence of vinyl is teaching us something about a need in our own hearts and souls.

Records have grooves, the indentations in the vinyl that make a path for the needle of the record player to travel and produce sound. When a record skips, the problem is typically in the groove, some dust or dirt that is preventing the needle from traveling its prescribed path.

Human hearts also have grooves, indentations that hold the chambers—the atria and the ventricles—together. Records and hearts have so much in common: grooves, beat, rhythm. They are easily broken and bent and difficult to mend. They are fragile and strong at the same time.

I come from the era of the Walkman, the boom box, the cassette tape radio alarm clock, the Discman. I knew a lot about recording, how you must press record and play simultaneously to snag your favorite song off the radio. I learned that some cassette tapes were designed to prevent people from recording over them. I learned that sermon tapes from church were made like this. I may or may not have recorded rap and R&B music over my mom's sermon tapes by placing a thin strip of Scotch tape over the top right and left corners of the cassette. As she reads this, it may or may not be my mom's first time finding out whatever happened to our pastor's sermon on the prodigal son that she could never seem to find. Hi, Mom.

I learned that my boom box was awesome at recording, but I didn't know my soul was also good at it and that my heart would remember all the things that would ever break it. Most recordings have a way of fading over time and losing their quality, but the moments that become the record our souls keep manage to stay so vivid. They pile on top of one another each time we get rejected, every time someone uses their words against us, any time our hearts get broken. It builds a record inside of us that tells us who and what we can be.

My husband and I host a get-together at our home called The Listening Party. We gather with our creative and artistic friends for a potluck and album listening. For the first thirty minutes, we eat food and chat. Then we take our journals and sketchbooks and write or draw while we listen to an album from beginning to end, with no pauses and very little talking.

For our first listening party, we chose Outkast's *Aquemini*. We listened to Big Boi and André 3000 spin tales of Atlanta's streets, the thrill of falling in love, the rise and fall of gangsters, and the way to freedom. Some of us were hearing the album for the first time. Some knew the songs they'd heard on the radio but had never listened to the album in its entirety. Some of us had heard the album repeatedly, but it had been a long time since we'd listened to the whole thing without distraction.

Aquemini was the soundtrack to my freshman year of college. Its bass line lifted from car windows like smoke from an abandoned cigarette. Its staccato drums wafted from dorm room windows like the scent of fresh laundry. For those of us who were just arriving in Atlanta for college, *Aquemini* was our official welcome to the city, and that welcome was warmly written by two of the city's most well-known sons.

The songs on the album still remind me of all the excitement and uncertainty of my first year of undergrad. The freedom of living life without my mom to check on where I was going and who I was going with. The responsibility of managing time, money, and my own boundaries. Feeling grown-up for the first time, while not really knowing what it meant to be truly grown-up in the first place.

In the 1990s, it seemed like hip-hop could only be East Coast or West Coast. Outkast proved that hip-hop could be Southern too. Listening that night, now years later, I could see *Aquemini* not just as an album of nostalgia, but I could hear the genius way Outkast took their Southern upbringing, heritage, and roots and poured them into a hip-hop record. While I listened, I thought about the Southern roots I came from and wrote a poem about them.

Start with your roots
Back porch
Harmonica
Washboard
Rhythm of picking beans

Grandma saying "close the screen door behind you"
It's okay to be proud to be from the South
To rep for hot summers
Cobbler and watermelon sticky fingers
Big mama and grandpa
Mamaw and papaw
To never wish for better luck or four leaf clovers
Because New Year's and black-eyed peas and collard greens
Because an itch in the palm of your hand means a payday
    is coming
Because an itch on the nose means a surprise visitor is coming
Because you protect yo mama's back when you don't step on
    a crack
Because when you see gray hair, you say yes ma'am, no ma'am,
    yes sir, no sir
Because no matter how old you are, you respect your mama's
    house
Grandma's hands
And kisses on mama's cheeks
Dirt under granddad's fingernails from tending his garden
Daddy smelling like homemade oil changes and pork chops
Take that with you
Carry it
Wrapped in wax paper like grandma's chicken and chocolate
    cake
Take it in the car, on the bus, on the train, on the plane
Remember why she does this
Remember she knows the sting of sit in the back, of colored
    sections, colored entrance, colored water fountains

The long wait on road trips between stops and countertops
that may not serve your kind here
She wraps food in wax paper the same way she hopes her
prayers caress the brown skin of her children and
children's children
To keep them safe from noose and bullet and eyes and hands
filled with hate
Take that with you
Read it on crinkly pages
Like the family Bible with records of deaths and births and
weddings and generations
Breathe it in
Like the scent of candied yams
And rain coming
And magnolia trees, pig smokers, and fried everything
Hold it in your chest
Like grandma's voice singing it is well
Like granddaddy giving thanks
And holding hands at the head of the table
From there
You can grow
Become your own tree
Spread your branches and limbs
Make your own generations
Create a safe place
To lean on
And find shade
Be spring, embrace summer, fall but always survive winter
Bloom

Then plant seeds
So they'll be here long after your tree ceases to go through
    the seasons
Start with your roots and always return there.

After the last track played, each of us shared what we liked about the record, what made us comfortable or uncomfortable, what inspired us, the questions we wanted to ask. The Listening Party reminded me of when I got my first boom box, how I couldn't wait to lie on the floor in my room and listen to an entire CD or cassette, how some stories are meant to be experienced in total with no interruptions.

In the same way we build our own internal assortment of music entangled with memories, our soul builds its own collection of records comprised of the words people have said to us, the words we say to ourselves, the things we believe about God.

In our souls is a massive record collection. Melodies, rhythms, bass lines, messages, lies, and truth that we've amassed along the way. Depending on what we've recorded, our hurts, wounds, and failures move the needle to the record we're used to playing, to berate ourselves when we fail or when life doesn't meet our expectations.

We are constantly recording. I don't mean in the way we hide behind our smartphones and tablet screens, trying so desperately to capture a moment to view later versus experiencing it in the present. I mean our hearts and souls are constantly recording.

I still remember the first boy who told me I was pretty. The warm brownies I had the night of my first kiss. The chime of the ice cream truck in the summer. The taste of my stepmother's cornbread dressing. The hardwood floors and wooden pews in my grandmother's church. The Tramaine Hawkins gospel music my mom played whenever she'd had a bad day. The worn leather in my great-grandfather's station wagon.

I can also remember the full name of the first junior high kid who teased me. I can still feel the nervousness caged in my chest after my parents divorced, when my child-self realized I missed my dad but didn't have the language to articulate it. The sting of my college professor's criticism that made me question if I'd ever become a writer. The blaring message that I wasn't worthy of love repeating itself with every noncommittal guy I dated. I carried those fears into my engagement to my husband, worrying if I had what it took to sustain a marriage if my parents were unable to.

For you, it may be the cutting words of an ex, the criticism of a parent, being passed over for a promotion, or the betrayal of someone you thought was a friend.

You're not good enough. You'll never be good enough. You don't belong here.

We are constantly recording.

Everyone has messages like these that rattle around in our minds and rise to the surface of our feelings at the most inopportune times. These repeating words keep us from speaking up, from standing up for what's right, from loving and being loved, from pursuing our dreams, and from growing in our relationship with God.

No matter where you're from, how much money you make, how old you are, your social or relationship status, everyone has his or her own stack of broken records. It's hard to fix a broken record. We can try to use our will, our good deeds; we can try to keep up appearances in hopes that they will be the glue that holds us together. But the only way to fix our broken records is to examine what we have recorded there and trust the God who makes broken things whole to heal our faulty recordings and replace them with true and hopeful ones.

CHAPTER 35

Finding Your Voice

Telling someone how to find their voice is like telling someone the exact moment they will feel comfortable in their skin. It just doesn't work that way. Both journeys are piece by piece, a winding path of learning to care about ourselves, about what we think and say, which will in turn make us want to honor the voices and thoughts of those around us.

For as long as I can remember I've wanted to be a writer. Okay, that's not entirely true. When I was five, I wanted to be the president of a bank because I thought I'd be able to keep all the money for myself. From six to eight years old, after watching the video of Whoopi Goldberg's one-woman Broadway show and sneaking to watch as much of Eddie Murphy's *Delirious* on VHS as I could without getting caught, I wanted to be a comedian. But at nine years old in Mrs. Perry's class, I discovered I wanted to be a writer.

I grew up in a house full of books. My mom, an avid reader, kept all of her books on a large wall unit in our living room, and I vowed to read them all, even the ones I was too young to understand. She and my grandmother took me to greeting card stores, bookstores, and the library. As a kid, I would much rather sit in the corner with a good book than play outside. As an adult, I would much rather sit in the corner with a good book than go outside.

Mrs. Perry read us poetry, and then she handed us cardboard, duct tape, and blank sheets of paper and told us to write our own poetry. She has no idea how much she changed my life that day. We spent the week using markers and colored pencils, writing our poetry on pages and drawing illustrations for our books. My friend Porsha brought her mom's dish towels to school for both of us to use as our book covers. I never thought to ask Porsha if her mom had actually given her permission to take a nice dish towel and duct tape it to a piece of cardboard forever. I had ten pages all to myself to write whatever came to my mind. My nine-year-old self somehow knew I'd want to do that for the rest of my life.

In the mid-1990s, I discovered hip-hop for myself. I had heard hip-hop music all my life. I had watched Run DMC tear down the wall figuratively and literally in their iconic music video for "Walk This Way," knew all the words to Salt-N-Pepa's "Push It," wanted my own verse on "Ladies First" right next to Queen Latifah and Monie Love. My interest in poetry became this great connection to my love for hip-hop music. I realized Lauryn Hill, Nas, and Black Thought were poets just as much as Shakespeare was. They were writing in the common vernacular and telling the story of the people, the community, the streets—stories of love, danger, betrayal, classism, sexism, and racism.

Everything changed for me when the movie *Love Jones* came out. Larenz Tate played a spoken-word artist named Darius, who falls in love with Nina, played by Nia Long. Seeing Darius spit his free-verse poetry over the timbre of that upright bass was the first time I knew that the rhythm and wordplay I loved in hip-hop verses and the beautiful language I'd read in so many poetry books could be combined into one art form.

In college, I performed at hole-in-the-wall open mics. After college, I performed at Christian worship events, conferences, churches, and youth events. There, I learned to feel responsible for my voice, to honor the moments I stood in front of an audience of people and spoke about the hope and light of God. These moments were not about anyone knowing my name or getting any amount of renown; these moments were about lifting the name of God and becoming a clear conduit for the truth of God.

As what I thought would always be a hobby transitioned into a career of performing poetry at faith-based events, I stayed drawn to open mics and the poetry community. After years of performing in mostly Christian spaces, I returned to Java Monkey Speaks, a Sunday night weekly open mic still held in Decatur, Georgia. I performed my poems there, but my work and my soul felt disconnected from the very scene that taught me so much about performance and writing.

After a few weeks, Megan, one of the frequent readers at Java Monkey Speaks, and I met for the first time. I was familiar with her work and admired how her poetry combined the wordplay of English academia with the deadpan, sarcastic voice of MTV's animated character Daria.

"Amena," she said, "when I hear other poets' work, I feel like I get to know them. But when I hear your work, I don't see you. I don't get to know you."

Her words haunted me when I went home that night. Had I come to believe that if my work was honoring God, I had to become invisible? Would the God who took painstaking measures to create me uniquely want that same unique creation to be unseen? In Megan's sentences, I heard a call for storytelling, for what so many of my English teachers called "showing and not telling."

I was comfortable telling about God, using the preachiest voice I could muster, but ask me to "show" God and it was a struggle. I had implicitly learned that to express God in my poetry, I shouldn't tell any stories about myself. I should cover up and keep my humanity from showing.

In many church settings, as a speaker, leader, and performing artist, I was taught that if God is to be seen, I must be invisible. As a woman, and particularly as a woman of color, I had many moments where I was seen as invisible by others, as overlooked, ignored, or dismissed. In my journey with Jesus, I'm learning that, like many marginalized women he encountered, Jesus sees me, and that God's ability to be seen isn't dependent on my ability to diminish who he made me to be.

I took Megan's feedback as a good challenge. I began to search my neighborhood, my family, and my soul for stories. I found them everywhere: in the breakup conversation at the table across from me at the coffee shop, in the way my grandma taught my dad to play the piano, in the story of how I fell in love, in my struggles with faith and doubt.

I learned that God, as the inventor of Story, is the best storyteller there is, that God's voice doesn't need my invisibility to shine. That God is bigger than that. God doesn't need me to step out of the way so he can shine his glory. God is no flashlight, no stage light, no sun or moon. God shines bigger than that, and nothing and no one will keep him from shining. He shines how he wants to, when he wants to. He shines in his creation;

he shines in the beauty and in the ugliness. He shines if what I write explicitly mentions his name; he still shines if it doesn't.

God taught me a lot through the things Megan said. I learned to stop hiding behind religious clichés or convenient platitudes. I learned to be my full self, to let my voice emerge as I lived and learned and loved and hurt. I learned to trust God to do the shining in and through me and to not put so much pressure on myself. I'm still learning.

I've been performing poetry for more than half my life. What started out as hip-hop-inspired free verse mixed with the traditional poetry I studied in college has transformed into the combination of poetry and monologue that I perform as spoken word today.

Sometimes I have begrudged my voice, wished it were edgier, wished my rhyme scheme were as tightly written as hip-hop taught me it should be, wished I had something more shocking or controversial to say. But the words that come to me are about soul, soil, goofy things I've realized over the years, a small attempt to describe a big God. My words are hope and wondering. My writing is question marks that never intended to become periods. My voice is the courage and determination of my ancestors, the rebellion of my generation, the joy I learned from sitting around the table and laughing with my family.

I want to speak with confidence that the only reason I stand here is because of the God who called me, gave me this gift, and sent me here. I want to stand strongly and speak boldly, as so many women and men before me have done. I want to feel no need to apologize for who I am, what my story is, or where I come from, because all those things have created the loved, imperfect woman I am today.

At this point in my life, there is a settling in me. I hate the word *settle*, as in settling for second best or settling for less. But this is a different kind of settling. It's a settling that brings rest. It's not the kind of comfort that keeps you resistant to change; it's the kind of comfort you find in someone's eyes when you know you are loved. The kind of comfort I find in stillness with God.

I am settled in carrying the responsibility of how I use my voice and the influence I'm given. To remember every community has and needs its poets. The job of a poet is to be a prophet, and it is not the job of the prophet to only say the things that make people happy and comfortable. Sometimes poets must say the hard things, must bring up the sadness and anger lingering beneath people's sentences and actions, must dismantle word by word and brick by brick the systems that oppress anyone who bears the image of God.

Finding your voice takes time. It takes realizing that everything—the sound of the drive to your grandma's house, the wounds of war in a nation or in your soul, the smell of your dad's cologne, your first heartbreak, your roommate's favorite song—is at all times creating your voice.

And even the voice I've found so far could be so different ten years from now. Wherever I am in life, I want to accept where my voice is and know that my voice and I are on a journey together, and the words are written to remind me where I've been and where I'm headed next.

CHAPTER 36

God Is in
the Groove

I recently became reacquainted with a song I now know changed my life: "Watermelon Man" by Herbie Hancock. As the daughter of a keys and bass player who loved fusion jazz, I knew Herbie Hancock's name, but I mostly associated him with what always felt like the diluted jazz of the late 1970s and early 1980s. This changed when I decided to take a History of Jazz course in college.

Professor Joe Jennings glided into class. I recognize the use of the word *glide* in that sentence, and I know exactly what I'm doing by using this word as a description for how Professor Jennings walked. He didn't step. He didn't strut. There was nothing overexaggerated or pretentious about the way he transitioned into a room. He glided.

He wore all black—not mournful all black, or goth all black, but cool, smoky, beret and goatee all black. He leaned back in a way that made me expect the bottom of his black slacks to be belled, but they were tapered right above the sole line of his shiny black shoes.

He looked at all of us, surveying our seriousness, silliness, studiousness. He introduced himself and let us know if we were looking for an easy A kind of class, we had signed up for the wrong elective.

"This is History of Jazz," he said, "and you will be learning and doing work in this class. What do y'all think jazz is?"

"Smooth, background, relaxing, elevator music," some students volunteered.

"Brass, bass, horns," others suggested.

Professor Jennings pressed play on his old-school record/tape/CD player, and the frenetic sounds of a bebop record entered our classroom. After a couple of minutes, he turned it off and said, "Does that sound relaxing to you? Like background or elevator music?"

We shook our heads no.

"What about this?" he said and played a jazz song with what seemed like an everlasting, solemn horn riff. "Yeah, that's jazz too."

He handed each of us a cassette tape. Yeah, a cassette tape—the one that had to be rewound and would not go gentle into that good night of your MP3 player or computer playlist.

"Listen to this and write what you think in a paper. You have one week."

When I put that tape into my old, faithful boom box and heard "Watermelon Man," it started off so strangely, sounding like a combination of a quintet of Coke bottle blowers with some yelps mixed in. Then one of the funkiest grooves I'd ever heard in my entire life slithered its way through that Coke bottle sound, added a layer of tastefully placed guitar, and I realized two things: there was more to Herbie Hancock than what I'd heard or assumed and jazz was bigger and better than I had imagined.

That song changed my life because I realized it's possible for art to broaden your idea of what's possible, inexplicably touch your soul, express something you can't and don't want to put words to, and create this visceral response in your hands, chest, hips, and neck. Because of Herbie Hancock's "Watermelon Man," I'm forever in search of that verb, phrase, art, bass line, rhyme—groove that can help me better define or refine the feelings, thoughts, and emotions deeply connected to our human experience.

God wants to use the bass line in my mom's prayers, the cello in my sister's laugh, the record scratch in my husband's voice first thing in the morning, to remind me of who he is. To remind me that sometimes the best thing I can do is get in the groove with God. Let the groove make me dance, make me cry, make me contemplate. Let the groove remind me that God's got soul, rhythm, and the best intentions for my life. That this God worthy of giving my life to isn't predictable. Isn't confined to a three-point sermon or a chorus-verse-chorus-bridge worship song. Isn't confined to humanity, although he fully embodied humanity and divinity. That God is in the unexplainable, in the mystery of how the groove of a perfect bass line teaches my hips to dance and my arms to sing.

Find God in the groove, in the change, in the challenge, in the healing, in the waiting, in the anticipating. When you find God's groove, remember to dance. Whether it's a dirge or a second line, a praise you keep in your calf muscles or a song that makes its way from the depth of your soul to your lips. Look for

God in the dance, in the song, in the poem. Look for God in the masterpiece he is always composing on leaves and in sunsets and from the notes of a salsa horn section.

Hear the truth. Hear the hope. Hear the peace Jesus brings with him into every record you've got playing in your life. Lies don't get to play on repeat here. There's healing in the melody. You can find a new song here. Put your ear to the groove and listen.

Liner Notes

To Bill Jensen, thank you for viewing your literary agency as a ministry; for talking me through all my misgivings as I approached what felt like the mountain of writing my next book; for all the conversations about food and music; for all the meetings, emails, prayers, and talks that led to this book idea I really cared about coming to fruition.

To Carolyn McCready, I knew when I sat across the table from you and we talked about the power of words and the importance of biscuits that I'd enjoy working with you. Thank you for believing in my voice and supporting me every step of the way as an editor and as a friend.

To Bridgette, Tom, Jennifer, Lori, Dirk, and the other members of the Zondervan/HarperCollins Christian Publishing team whom I didn't have the chance to meet—thank you for partnering with me to help give this book strong wings to fly.

To Andrea Vinley Converse, because of you I permanently keep a box of tissues on my desk when I write. You made me feel like I wasn't doing it right if I wasn't crying sometimes.

Thank you for all the pep talks, for being honest even when I told you I thought the job of a writing coach was to tell me I'm amazing all the time. LOL. Thanks for all the times you said "No, you *have* to write that," when it was hard, hurtful, or uncomfortable. Thanks for the chocolate and suggestions of where to eat quality carbs. This book is the best it could be in part because of you.

To JR Montes, it's a rare combination to find someone in a booking agent and manager who encourages an artist to not just take opportunities for the money, but to be true to creativity and artfulness and to make family and taking care of oneself a priority. You are that rare combination. You have walked alongside Matt and me and partnered with us as we've developed our sound, as I've found my voice, as that voice has changed as I've grown and developed as an artist and a writer. Thanks for listening to all my long voice mails, for that night Matt and I sat at the dinner table with you and Melissa right before what was about to be not only one of the toughest times in my life but the toughest time in the process of working on this book. For you and your wife looking at both of us and letting us know in so many ways that we could survive this. And we did. Here's to more dreaming, more doing, and more talking hip-hop.

To Michelle Norris, for the fantastic author photo and styling—here's to me wearing clothes that actually fit. HA! To Giselle Grant, for the fabulous show hair 'do, for always taking such good care of my curls, and for all the conversations we have that are so good for my soul. To Bee Wade, for helping me to serve face so well in the author photos.

To my community of writers, creatives, and leaders who talked me through so much of what is written here: Nish, Preston,

Seth, Adrienne, Kimberly, Adan, Ashlee, Jess, Andie, Elora, Ann, Jo, Latasha, Helen, Vivian, Kathy, Deidra, Austin, Leigh, Candi, Angie, Sandra, Robin, Katie, Juliet, and insert-your-name-here-if-i-forgot-and-charge-it-to-my-head-and-not-my-heart-because-I-love-you. ☺ Thank you for your words, perspective, grit, humor, prayers, sounding board, support, community, accountability, pushback, and push-forward. Thank you for the ways you are all yourselves in the world and the ways you encourage me to be the same.

To my family, for your unending belief in me and support of me. For celebrating with me and walking me through the times that were hard to celebrate. For all the tables and good food we share. For making me LAUGH and keeping me humble. You are what love looks, sounds, and feels like. I love you all!

To my husband and my favorite deejay, you know the stories here through and through. You lived many of them with me; you heard me recount them; you watched me wrestle with writing them; you brainstormed with me; you took me out for donuts when I was spent from a day of crying and writing. You are my partner in everything, and God has used you to fix so many of my broken records. We've got so much more art to make and so much more life to live. Here's to matching Adidas suits, driving through ATL, bumping Outkast with the windows down on a warm, spring day. I love you. Always.

My biggest shout-out always goes to you, Jesus. It's weird to write acknowledgments to you because you know what I'm thinking anyway. Also, a paragraph, poem, page, or book just ain't gonna do justice to articulating all that you are to me. Somehow, beyond my brain's ability to understand, you save; you redeem; you speak truth; you give grace; and you love. Thank you for using this book to teach me how to just be myself, to do what you've given me to do and trust you to do the rest.

To everyone who read, bought, and shared this book. Thank you. Seriously thank you. It was great meeting you. Let's find some more of those little key lime pie Snickers dessert things and talk about the new records you're listening to. I can't wait to hear all about it.